Finding My Banana Bread Man

Finding My Banana Bread Man

a journey through mourning

JOHN R. DAVIS

Finding My Banana Bread Man: A Journey Through Mourning

Copyright © 2008 John R. Davis. All rights reserved. No part of this book may be reproduced or retransmitted in any form or by any means without the written permission of the publisher.

Published by Wheatmark®
610 East Delano Street, Suite 104
Tucson, Arizona 85705 U.S.A.
www.wheatmark.com

International Standard Book Number:
978-1-60494-011-4
Library of Congress Control Number:
2007941150

All definitions taken from *The American Heritage Dictionary of the English Language*.

Excerpts from *Another Day in the Frontal Lobe* used with permission of the author.

Editing by Faye Quam Heimerl

Jack at Age Four

In loving memory of my partner and best friend, John "Jack" Edward Orler, who taught me how to live in the moment and how to die with grace. Jack continues to provide me with memories of green. He will always be my soft place to land.

Contents

Foreword ix
Author's Note xiii

1. Shock: Remembering the Start of the End of It All. 1
2. Recall: What the Heart Knows 13
3. Loss: He Was My Soft Place to Land 23
4. Frustration: A Good Man's Heart 35
5. Guilt: Crazy with Watching You Slip Away. . 49
6. Despair: Anchor Lost, Spirit Broken 61
7. Death: Memories of Green 73
8. Loneliness: Empty Is Silence 83
9. Searching: Recovery Spans a Lifetime. 97
10. Forgiveness: My Heart Will Have to Lead This Race. 105
11. Revelation: The Hummingbird's Sweet Smile 115
12. Remembrance: Always Mine ... Times Two 129
13. Hope: Finding My Banana Bread Man, Finding Myself 141

Epilogue. 155
Jack's Banana Bread Recipe 156
Memories of Green: Photographs. 159

Reflections

Writing This Book	185
About Brain Tumors	187
My Wish List	191
While Your Loved One Is Still with You	193
After Your Loved One Has Died	195
Sending News to "Jack's Gallery"	199
Requesting Help	203
Caregiver Instructions to Helpers	207
Analogy for Grief	211
Letter from Papa Jack to Madison and Mia	213
Dream: Leaving to Accept	217
My Father's Box	221
Letters to Jack	225
Others' Words About Grief	237
Victims or Victors?	241
Individuals Named in This Book	243
Acknowledgements	247
About the Author	251

Foreword

I first met John Davis late in October of 2005, on the Internet, when I read the first of many messages he would post on Hospice of the Valley's online Grief Healing Discussion Groups. His introductory piece was entitled "Remembering Jack," and his moving tribute to his beloved life partner touched the hearts of all who read it. In the days and weeks that followed, his honest, thoughtful, and insightful posts endeared him to everyone, as he became one of the most cherished and respected members of this close-knit, virtual support group.

From the beginning, I was struck by John's absolute determination to make his journey through grief a healing one, to move through it thoughtfully, and work with it deliberately. As the weeks and months went by, he discovered, utilized, and shared with the rest of us a wide variety of ideas, practices, and resources he'd found that helped him make sense of it all. He worked hard to understand both the grief he felt in anticipation of Jack's death, and the reactions he experienced afterward, as he mourned the physical loss of his mate. He was struggling to find a way to live in this world in the absence of his beloved, while still maintaining a connection with him. Finally, he made a decision to find his partner once again: by remembering him, by discovering the soulful legacies he left behind, by finding meaning in his death, and by deliberately choosing to live a better life in his honor. In the process of finding him, John pays fitting tribute to his beloved Jack by writing this book, in which he shares openly and honestly with his readers what he has learned about love, loss, and grief.

In my own experience with loss and in my work with the bereaved, I am absolutely convinced that the more we learn about grief, the better we are able to cope with it. Although the experience is unique to each of us, grief is a normal, natural response to loss that, depending on how it is managed, can lead to healing and personal growth. John's story is a very personal account of one man's journey through grief, but because he shares so generously the important discoveries he makes along the way, his experiences serve as a helpful guide to other mourners, and they offer hope to those who find themselves on a similar path.

I am especially appreciative of John's passionate defense of his need not to "let go" of Jack, despite all the unsolicited advice and encouragement he received from certain friends and family members to do exactly that. As a bereavement counselor, I often encounter individuals who torture themselves in the mistaken belief that they should "find closure" by "letting go" of their loved ones who have died, and say good-bye to them forevermore, but intuitively, we know that letting go of someone we love so dearly is the last thing in the world we want to do, and we resist it with every fiber in our being. In recent years, this notion of "letting go" of one's at-

Foreword

tachment to the deceased loved one has given way to a more enlightened view of bereavement. Today we acknowledge that good memories can be powerful sources of comfort and very real points of connection to the deceased. We now recognize that maintaining emotional bonds with a loved one who has died can enrich the life of the person who survives.

In finding his mate and remembering his finest qualities, John has found a way to keep Jack's spirit alive, not only for John himself but for others who knew and loved him, too, influencing who they are now, and who they will become in the future. In this way, their connection remains unbroken, and their love will endure forever. John's book is testimony to the fundamental truth that love never dies.

Respectfully Yours,
        Martha Tousley—APRN, BC, FT,
        certified Fellow in Thanatology:
        Death, Dying and Bereavement

Author's Note

Several years ago, Jack and I had been busily people watching on Duval Street, Key West, Florida, when we noticed a bedraggled old man riding past us on his bicycle, its large basket stacked with loaves of homemade banana bread. As he pedaled, he sang, "Banana bread man, banana bread man! Get it now, or don't blame me when it's gone!" Clearly, he was a regular on this street, because person after person called his name and waved him down. He traded his bread, stories, and laughter for dollars.

I imagined that, like this man, Jack ferried his baked goods in the basket of a bike. As a young man of 15, *My* Banana Bread Man, Jack Orler, also sold banana bread. Every week, from 1964 through 1966, he fired up his mother's oven to bake 80 loaves of bread, which he then sold to grocers in the rural town of Norway, Michigan, located about 100 miles north of Green Bay, Wisconsin, on Michigan's Upper Peninsula.

Jack made baking bread into a successful business, and was able to purchase his first car with his earnings. He applied his entrepreneurial skills to the rest of his businesses, too, his last, a thriving hair salon in Fountain Hills, Arizona. Everything he touched turned to gold. His personal life, *and* his beautiful hair, were as golden as his finances.

I supposed Jack didn't have anything in common with the Key West man, other than selling banana bread. They certainly didn't look alike. Jack was fastidious about his appearance, and this man was scruffy.

Later that day, though, he passed us again, singing. His basket was empty, but people were still stopping him. Seeing that he'd sold all his bread, I was convinced he shared Jack's knack for sales, as well as his magnetism, openness, and ability to draw friends to himself. Yes, Jack knew how to make friends.

On the first day of Norway's 1964-65 school year, Jack's grade had an influx of new students. He was aware these kids wouldn't know anyone, so, as his first-hour homeroom class assembled, he acted as class goodwill ambassador, weaving words of welcome in and around the new and returning students. (In a matter of weeks, he would become friends with all of them.) Displaying his banana-bread-man personality, he offered his hand to new students, saying, "Hello, I'm Jack Orler," then he directed them to look out the window. He pointed across the street, and said, "I live right over there, in the house with the red roof."

Jack's personality developed in 1964, and expanded and blossomed throughout his remaining 41 years. It became his trademark, his philosophy for navigating life. He consistently extended his hand in friendship, fostering warmth in whomever he touched. I, a truly lucky man, was a beneficiary of 27 years of his friendship, warmth, and love.

Author's Note

Late July 2005, I lost Jack to cancer. I lost myself, too. I wondered, *Is it possible to live without him, after relying on his physical presence, his way of making life more colorful?*

I mourned Jack, I wanted him back, but I didn't know where he was. So I began to search for him. I picked up my pen and began writing poetry, letters, and this book, *Finding My Banana Bread Man*. I began my journey through mourning.

1.

Shock: Remembering the Start of the End of It All

"Without surgery, you have six to eight weeks to live," Jack's surgeon, Dr. Frederick Marciano, said matter-of-factly. "With it, you might live another twelve to eighteen months." (Dr. Marciano was a surgeon who operated on U.S. Army Private Jessica Lynch after she was released from captivity in Iraq.) "I can perform the surgery here, or you can have someone else do it, over at Barrows Neurological Institute."

Every event in Jack's life seemed to proceed with lightning speed and fanfare, and the onset and diagnosis of his illness was no exception. In September 2004, he experienced two weeks of headaches. And then, in a matter of days, he saw a doctor, a specialist, and he received a CAT scan, followed by the blunt and morbid news that he had a glioblastoma multiforme (GBM) grade IV brain tumor—the worst kind of brain tumor there is. Three days later, October 5, he underwent surgery.

In the long moments after we received the diagnosis, I made my way out of Jack's hospital room and into the corridor, where two of our dear friends Penny and Marion were keeping vigil. Seeing them, I fell to my knees and sobbed, "I feel like I'm in a deep hole with the earth collapsing on me." I'd just been jolted by the despair that accompanies a death sentence—also known as brain cancer. The pendulum of my emotions had been set in motion, and, for the next 10 months, it would swing from fear to hope, sorrow to joy, from despair to determination. I had seen the future, and I'll always remember the start of the end of it all.

Remembering the Start of the End of it All

Two times I witnessed what our future would hold
A slip, a trip, a stumble, and you fold
I reached out to grab you and lessen the fall
then we brushed it off: "It's nothing at all"

How could a man who's fit and strong
have his legs turn to jelly? It seemed so wrong
His headaches continued for days on end
Warnings and signals, yet they seemed pretend

Just a bad headache; that's the correct call
Do you remember the start of the end of it all?

The disposal was left rumbling, the switch still on
Disordered and scattered, the neat you left town
Your timely clean habits were eerily gone
The You that I knew was nowhere around

Just a bad headache; that has to be the call
Do you remember the start of the end of it all?

Finally, your head pounded day after day
then you required a medical CAT Scan, an x-ray

There in the smoke-colored film hanging on the wall
is THE TUMOR that instigated your fall

A massive brain tumor? That can't be the call!
Do you remember the start of the end of it all?

Anger, denial, and despair were there
Two months or two years with maximum care
Less than a year was reality's dish
Less than the lifetime that we had wished

A massive brain tumor. Yes, that was the call
Remember the start ... of the end of it all?

Oh, I remember the start of the end of it all
It's just a headache. That must be the call
You've less than a year left, was reality's dish
What about a lifetime, every lover's wish?

Now that I've witnessed the future told
The slip, the trip, the stumble, your fold
I reach out and grab for you, but you're not there
No You to brush off—No You, nowhere

Jack's surgery, performed by Dr. Peter Nakaji, at Barrows Neurological Institute, St. Joseph's Hospital and Medical Center, commenced at 4:00 p.m., October 5, and dragged on for 10 merciless hours, my agony interrupted only when friends or family members joined me in Jack's room, or when a nurse or doctor gave me a progress report. Four hours into the surgery, my younger sister Cathy, from Oregon, arrived; shortly after that, Jack's surgeon confirmed the diagnosis: glioblastoma multiforme grade IV tumor.

Jack had been in the operating room nine hours when I felt like I couldn't go on any longer. I felt dead. Before this night, I hadn't known it was possible to talk, breathe, and feel dead, all at the same time. Desperate for rest, Cathy and I left at 1:00 a.m., and drove to my house. We were worried about Jack, but exhaustion took over, and we were able to sleep.

We crept into his hospital room early the next morning, and we were unprepared for what we saw. Jack was not unconscious, but was sitting up in bed and sipping water! We couldn't believe how good he looked. I thought, *His hair! Jack still has all his hair!* Then I thought, *Can someone be awake and alert this soon after major brain surgery? How can this be? Amazing!* Seeing him in this condition gave me hope; after all, he still looked like my Jack. Being who he was, he would persevere. He was going to get well.

Our fear softened when the surgeons told us they'd removed all "they could see" of the cancer, a tumor the size of a tangerine. His prognosis looked good, and our mood improved. (Only two nights prior to this, we had cuddled in Jack's bed, and confessed to each other that we were terrified.)

Within 24 hours of surgery Jack was up and walking, and within 48 hours he was transferred out of the ICU. Good news. He was recovering quickly.

The surgeons removed all the tumor they could see, but that wasn't the same as removing all the cancer. In her book, *Another Day in the Frontal Lobe,* neurosurgeon Katrina Firlik writes about brain cancer that's hard to find: "Consider what would happen if, when you try to open a bag of un-popped popcorn, the bag rips wide open, scattering the entire contents across the kitchen floor. A good-sized pile would end up right at your feet, and the kernels would radiate out from there. The relatively focused part of the mess would be easy to clean up. Over the next few days, though, you would be amazed to discover individual kernels that had made it all the way under the dining room table or into the living room. That's what a glioblastoma [glioblastoma multiforme] is like. You can clean up the focused mess, but you know there are cells you can't see at first, far removed from the obvious focus."

We chose to believe Jack's case was an exception, that his surgeon had removed all the cancer. We were positive this illness was beatable; it had to be, with Jack as the captain of his recovery team.

On October 11, just six days after having major brain surgery, Jack was discharged from the hospital. His left side was slightly weak, and he had minor vision loss in his left eye—both, aftereffects of the surgery—but, with rehabilitation, he was expected to regain what he lost. The last thing he did before he left the hospital was call home to record a new voice message on our answering machine: *Hi. You've reached Jack and John. I'm home from the hospital now. Please bring food. John can't cook.*

Humor and Jack were inseparable. For example, shortly before his surgery, Jack's mob of well wishers was still in his room when he received a drug to help him relax. As he began to nod off, to float into another world, he opened his eyes and gazed at everyone. He squinted at Brenda, who was standing at the foot of his bed, and with a devilish smile he said, "So *this* is what it's like to be in Brenda's world."

I shouldn't have been surprised by this, but I was. Jack was about to be wheeled away to have a tumor cut out of his head, and he was thinking about us, trying to make us laugh. That was Jack. Always, Jack.

Once home, Jack continued to grow stronger, but then after two weeks, I noticed he seemed to weaken; he began to slightly drag his left foot. He walked just fine otherwise, so we didn't worry. We'd been taking regular walks, eating dinner at his son's house, and were contemplating purchasing a new car that could accommodate his slight disability.

Things were progressing well, but then on Friday morning, October 22, I was awakened by a scream. Jack had hit his head on the nightstand. He'd gotten out of bed and slipped on some pillows that were lying on the floor. He appeared to be fine, but I insisted on taking him to St. Joseph's Hospital, anyway. Since he'd already been a patient there, I believed the staff would be the best equipped of any to deal with him; besides, I needed reassurance that he would be okay, and that his fall wouldn't slow down his recovery.

> *Shock—Something that jars the mind or emotions as if with a violent blow; the disturbance of function, equilibrium, or mental faculties caused by such a blow.*

Jack and I walked side by side into the emergency room. Five hours later he was discharged, sitting in a wheelchair, because he was unable to walk. I questioned the emergency room doctor about Jack's declining capacities. "He's got brain swelling," she insisted. "This is common after his kind of surgery. Keep him on the prescription I gave you, and he'll be back to his old self in 24 to 48 hours. You'll see."

"Are you sure? I mean-"

"Really. The medication will reduce the swelling, and he'll be able to walk again in a day or two."

I was incredulous. She wanted a man, who had walked into the emergency room, to go home, unable to walk. At least three different times I pointed out this discrepancy to the emergency doctor and nurses, but a nurse said, "Mr. Davis, I'm sorry, but we need his bed. Here are his discharge papers. Just keep giving him his meds. He'll be fine."

So I took Jack home, even when my gut said not to, and, from then on, I repeatedly berated myself for my lack in judgment. *Why didn't I insist they keep him for at least observation? Why didn't I demand he be admitted, especially when I knew better?*

Jack's surgeon, Dr. Nakaji, hadn't been told about his worsening condition. Later he said, "Had I been informed of Jack's deteriorating ability to walk, I would not have allowed him to be discharged from the emergency room." I never blamed Dr. Nakaji because I knew none of this was his fault.

Once home, I settled Jack comfortably in bed. Exhausted, he fell asleep. At midnight I shook him a little, to wake him up so he could take his medication, but he didn't stir. I shook him harder. He still didn't stir. "Jack!" I yelled. No response. I called 911, and seven hours and several transfers between hospitals later, he was back in the hospital he'd *walked* into only 24 hours earlier.

Jack was admitted to the ICU on Saturday morning, October 23. I trailed him into his room, but a nurse said, "You have to leave," and, as I was in no condition to argue, I obeyed. I paced the halls adjacent to his room. I shook. I cried. I sobbed through phone calls to friends, until, finally, Dr. Nakaji rushed up to me. "I need your permission to place a second external shunt in the right side of Jack's head," he said. "It will empty into his abdomen. I have to drain the fluid away from his brain." He handed me a clipboard holding a Consent Form. "This is a last-ditch effort, and, I am sorry to say, he has a minimal chance of surviving. I suggest you prepare for the worst."

The love of my life had had a stroke at home and fallen into a coma. *I should have forced them to admit him!* The pendulum swung toward fear. The doctor had all but declared that Jack's death was certain.

I Saw the Master's Plan

I saw the Master's plan one day, right there on the floor
I saw my shadow on the ground, but I saw yours no more

I saw the two of us become a strong and loving trust
I saw your bold blond hair grow with gold dust
I saw you laugh and cry and build a home that we would share
I saw you laugh and heard your voice—"I love you"—in my ear

I saw in you the man I love, knew that from the start
I saw in you the man who knew just how to touch my heart
I saw in you an artist's hands, a talent oh so rare
I saw you twist and craft each lock of silvered ladies' hair

I saw the Master's plan one day, right there on the floor
I saw my shadow on the ground, but I saw yours no more

I saw you shape and mold a son the two of us would raise
I saw a father's love grow strong and shape this young man's ways
I saw this man's child run to you and call you Papa Jack
I saw her eyes light up with love as she rode on your back

I saw a strong and gentle man begin his final race
I saw him fight the ravages of cancer's ugly face
I saw him live each moment of his last days on this earth
I saw him draw his final breath for all that it was worth

I saw the Master's plan one day, right there on the floor
I saw my shadow on the ground, but I saw yours no more

I saw the winds of time and spaces carry you away
I saw the angels coming, and they would not let you stay
I saw the future we had built, absent, broken, and bare
I saw my shadow on the ground, the one without you there

I saw the Master's plan one day, right there on the floor
I saw my shadow on the ground, but I saw yours no more

My emergency room experience is a clarion call to all medical professionals to work toward correcting inefficiencies and understaffing in hospitals. It is also a warning to everyone seeking emergency room care: Do not leave an emergency room in worse condition than you were admitted! I was ill prepared to recognize what was happening to Jack, but the hospital staff would have not only been able to recognize his symptoms, but may have been able to act quickly, and prevent the life-altering effects of his stroke and coma.

This said, I still assume personal responsibility for my failure to be more aggressive with the hospital staff. My error in judgment was costly, and both Jack's and my life were forever changed because of it. I learned, up close and personal, what it meant to be an advocate for someone's care. I never again let a medical professional brush me off or discredit my concerns. Staff always knew I'd be around, looking after Jack. I had a reputation for "being in everyone's face" whenever, or wherever, his care was involved.

"Life begins on the other side of despair."
                              Jean-Paul Sartre

2.

Recall: What the Heart Knows

At exactly 8:30 p.m., on October 28, 1978, I saw Jack for the first time, and my life burst open. We were at a Halloween party in Escanaba, Michigan, my hometown. Jack was 29, I was 28. Jack was living in Norway, Michigan, so we traveled back and forth between our homes, but after a year of this, we decided to live together in Norway.

I'd had nil romantic involvements prior to Jack: 30 years ago it was impossible to "come out" in rural United States, and I lived in a *rural* area (pop. 15,000). Given this, I didn't have relationships with which to compare ours, but it was always clear to me that Jack possessed everything I wanted. I couldn't help being physically attracted to his blonde-and-boyish good looks and his Lucy Ricardo personality.

We were the antithesis of each other: I had dark hair and was shyly reserved. He was blonde and outgoing, the life of the party. Our contrasting appearances would earn us the label of "a real item." The dynamics in our relationship would evolve to resemble that of Fred and Ethel on "I Love Lucy," Jack being Ethel, and I, Fred.

When we met, Jack had been divorced for five months. He'd always known he was gay, but, like many people, he tried to blend in and be accepted by society, which meant giving up a part of himself. He married in 1968, and became a father in 1969, raising his son Tom in Norway. He remained married for nine and a half years, but then his fiercely independent side—and marital discord—won out, and he and his wife divorced.

Recall—To remember; recollect. The ability to remember information or experiences.

Jack was always brimming with energy. He was constantly on the go, and, unlike me, he never—I mean *never*—rested. I was laidback, a person who needed time for relaxation. But time changed both of us. I became more animated, and Jack became more mellow, and I think my sedate ways brought an element of calm to Jack's feisty and, sometimes, wild (crazy), chronically involved personality. I've heard it said that you eventually grow to become more like your mate. I agree.

What the Heart Knows

We met in October of seventy-eight
First physical attraction then "mental mates"
Opposite sometimes, but each one strong
We harmonized as we made a beautiful song

Italian lifeblood moved through our veins
Italy, the land of lovers and villas and lanes
Parma and Tuscany of trade makers' sons
Fashioned two children from Roman ones

Family traits repeat and show
We were young and on fire
The Heart Knows

Our early years exciting, romantic, wild
Passionate lovers had no room for the mild
Years did nothing to dampen our flame
We burned with passion, some envied our claim

Family traits repeat and show
Two strong men of heritage
The Heart Glows

Destiny moved us from hometowns then West
Success always followed us; you never could rest
Patiently seeking and crafting a life
Creating a home full of laughter and light

Family traits repeat and show
So sure of the future
The Heart Grows

For years we toiled, created our space
Unaware of a destiny with cruel cancer's face
On the verge of triumph, one step from the wire
The angels grabbed you and left me on fire

Family traits repeat and show
Bleeding and broken
The Heart Unfolds

In memory's playground you're strong and tall
The weakness is gone, so is blindness and all

Gone are false visions, those delusions you saw
Replaced by memories that I lovingly recall

Caught in a nightmare, then you're physically gone
I find you at slumber with your smile's light still on
You're in your granddaughters' eyes, ears, and souls
Death Cannot Steal What The Heart Knows

Jack and I lived in Norway for one year, then moved to Milwaukee, Wisconsin, where we stayed for six months. In 1981, we moved back to Norway because Jack's father had died of lung cancer, and we wanted to watch over his mother. We purchased a mobile home tucked away in an ocean of oaks, at the end of a 400-foot driveway, on 10 acres of land. As if this setting wasn't beautiful enough, we added on to our house, then transformed it into a showpiece.

In 1985, we moved to Scottsdale, Arizona, where I took a job as Adjustment Deputy for the Unemployment Insurance Agency with the State of Arizona. Jack purchased the "Self Indulgence" hair salon in Fountain Hills, which he eventually renamed "Jack's Self Indulgence." We purchased a home in Scottsdale, not far from Fountain Hills, which we updated, upgraded, and added every conceivable amenity to until it would have been fit to be featured in *House Beautiful* magazine.

In September of 1989, we adopted a black and tan miniature dachshund we named Dusky. Jack gave him to *me*, as a birthday gift, but he always claimed

Dusky was *his*. Of course, this was Jack. I told people there was a pecking order in our household: Jack was first, Dusky second, and I was last. Alas, I accepted my position ... and enjoyed Dusky as a sweet, loving facet of our relationship.

On April 15, 1999, we moved into our dream home that we'd had built. Jack lived there for five years, three months, and sixteen days. Jack died there, too. Oh my, he loved that house! He loved me!

I've been asked why Jack loved me, and I think one reason was I had the ability to adapt to simplicity, the core reality of his life, which I didn't realize was his core reality until nine months after his death. From the outside, Jack appeared complex, but he had been clandestinely living a simple internal life. He required little to be happy. In an e-mail note to his son Tom, I shared my thoughts about this simplicity:

> Do you know what your dad told one of his customers just two weeks before he quit his business? He said, 'You know, I'm 99.9 percent happy with my life.' I'm not sure what they'd been talking about, but for anyone to make that type of comment and be that happy with their life is truly amazing. How many people do you know who can attribute that high of a percentage of happiness to their life? Personally, I know of none. Someday I hope to say I am 99.9 percent happy (as Jack did)—a daunting task without his physical presence.

I know Jack did not love me for the money I brought to the table (I had a good job, but he earned 70 percent of our income, a good income), but, rather, he loved that I was productive with a purpose. I always worked, and I don't think he could have remained involved with someone who did not have some purpose to his life. Money meant little to Jack, but being "productive with purpose" was essential.

Around the time Jack was diagnosed with cancer, he was in the process of dismantling his hair salon—which he owned and operated—not because his business was failing but because the strip mall in which his salon was located was being renovated, and the developers wouldn't commit to a new lease for Jack's salon. He saw their reticence as an opportunity to change how he did business: he sold his salon equipment, rented a chair in another salon, and told his devoted customers where to find him. He'd decided he could earn just as much profit as before, if not more, if he eliminated overhead and focused solely on styling hair.

This was also an opportune time for Jack to cut down on his hours and head into semi-retirement. I'd already retired from my position as a Call Center Manager with the State of Arizona, so we expected his reduced hours would give us more leisure time together. We enjoyed his new schedule for five months. I then returned to the Unemployment Insurance Agency, as a seasonal employee, but I quit for good after Jack got sick, and I haven't worked since. I needed to care for Jack during his illness, and, after his death, I needed to grieve. (I can't imagine how anyone can work and grieve at the same time. I know people do it, because society demands they act like robots, and hide their sadness. I know quitting work was the best thing for me.)

Now I do what I love to do: write. It's therapeutic, it helps me recall the man I love, and it brings him closer to me.

You're Filling The Shell Of This Man With Your Love

You bent, shaped, and twisted me, My Love
You forged me forever, severed what's rough
creating the new me and naming our love
You saw in the pieces a man you could love
You filled up the shell of this man with your love

Building our life took so many years
Then in a moment you ... are not here

Molten and foreign each element was
but when we were created our structure was tough
Moments and pictures, adventures we shared
long walks and movies were every day's fare
You filled up the shell of this man with your love

Weak is each substance, how strange is this stuff
but when blended together we called it Love
Tears and laughter and years flew by
because we knew tomorrow was ours on the fly
As you filled up the shell of this man with your love

Building our life took so many years
Then in a moment you ... are not here

Our foundation shaken, it fell to the ground
Ten months of illness would steal your sound
Blindness and heartache replaced what we'd found

And tears became everyday symbols around
But I was full, this shell of a man, with your love

Building our life took so many years
Then in a moment you ... are not here

I'll continue the process you taught me, for years
I'm bending and shaping and twisting, My Dear
I'll forge on forever, and sever what's rough
creating the new me first found in your love
You still fill the shell of this man with your love

Building our life took so many years
Then in a moment you ... are not here

Memories of you dance in my mind
but sorrow and pain I often still find
I see in the pieces that man that you loved
molten and foreign as each element was
Please fill up the shell of this man with your love

Building our life took so many years
Then in a moment you ... are not here

I'll continue the process you taught me, for years
I'm bending and shaping and twisting, My Dear
I'll forge on forever, and sever what's rough
creating the new me first found in your love
I fill the shell of this man with your love

When the summer of 2004 started easing into fall, Jack was alive and present, healthy and vibrant. We'd found time for two summer vacations, one to Michigan and the other to Colorado. In late August, we took a road trip, reaching out to Reno, Nevada, and circling back through Oregon. I remember feeling Jack's closeness as we stood, mesmerized, looking across clear Lake Tahoe, and as our eyes traced nature's crisp outlines along Crater Lake. Both places reflected an image of a god, who, I believe, is only capable of creating magnificence.

After visiting Crater Lake, we wound our way along the Pacific Coast Highway and into the majestic redwood forests of Northern California, and then back to Lake Tahoe, the two lakes acting as bookends for a trip dedicated to nature. This was fitting for my last trip with Jack. A fitting end to the life we shared.

Looking back to the night I met Jack, I don't think I could have imagined what was in store for me. I started that evening, in October 1978, alone, unattached, and living in a residence I shared with no one; I ended it having met the man who would change me forever, with whom I would share my life.

He was wearing a winter vest that night. It was navy blue and lined with red plaid flannel. It still hangs in my closet.

"God gave us memories that we might have roses in December."
James M. Barrie

3.

Loss: He Was My Soft Place to Land

While My Banana Bread Man lie in a coma, dying, I held his hand and pleaded with him. "Please don't leave me," I said. "Come back." This went on for two days, and then Jack granted my request: he came back to me. When I saw his eyes open, my pendulum swung toward elation. I sometimes wonder if his return had anything to do with my heartfelt calls to him.

Jack was now awake, but his left side was severely impaired and weakened by the stroke. We were certain extensive rehabilitation could take care of that, but we knew no amount of rehabilitation could remedy his loss of sight. In an instant, 90 percent of the world he surrounded himself with was taken away from him. His eyes would never look upon his son again. They would never look upon his granddaughter again. His beautiful brown eyes would never look upon *me* again.

The most devastating aspect of my journey through mourning had materialized: my Jack was going to have to live in a world of total darkness. It was apparent that, in the not too distant future, cancer would take Jack from me, and it was distressing that he was forced to live out his shortened life without the benefit of sight.

Added to my emotional pain was my understanding that blindness might not have had to be his companion. I thought, *If the emergency room had listened to me and kept him at the hospital, if I had more strongly insisted, no, demanded, he be admitted, this could have been prevented.*

Although unable to see, Jack's eyes still looked normal, natural, and perfect, the same as they always were: full, brown, and beautiful. Tragically, they now provided only darkness. Jack was experiencing cortical blindness: rather than his eyes, his optic nerve was affected. The area in his brain that controlled his sight had been 70 percent damaged, and the core of what caused it was deep, and disturbingly unfixable, within the delicate framework of his brain.

Jack, once vibrant, active, and healthy, a man who looked 15 years younger than his 55 years, had been transformed by cancer. Now, more than ever, he needed me to be his full-time advocate.

Loss—Something or someone that is lost. The harm or suffering caused by losing or by being lost. Setbacks. Destruction.

Jack looked younger than his age because he took great care of himself—yet another reason it was implausible that deadly cancer attacked him. He took vitamins daily, and was particularly attentive to his skin care and physical appearance. (He was in a profession which demanded this type of attention to one's appearance.) His 5'10" height and 165 pound weight were as ideal to me as everything else about his ageless persona.

Jack had meticulously styled blonde highlighted hair, worn a bit longer than is usually seen on a man of 55, but, given his youthful appearance, it suited him perfectly. If he had any hair loss, it was never apparent to me—I would have been conscious of its occurrence, having lost my own hair beginning at the age of 28. But, alas, his locks were shaved off when his surgeon placed a second shunt in his brain.

He Was My Soft Place To Land

I still remember, I still know
Where my eyes first saw his glow
I still see the distant land
Where I first saw that sweet man

I still recall the hair of gold
How it parted, how it glowed
I still see those eyes so brown
How they turned my heart around

He was my soft place to land
That sweet and gentle loving man

I'm not the only one to know
All the gifts he had to show
He showered them on many more
So much love he had to pour

He gave gifts of time and chat
For each heart that required time to yak
Recipes for life he scattered
Showing each what really mattered

Providing sage advice right from the heart
So popular right from the start
Always there to listen, too
The strength of what he was to you

He was my soft place to land
That sweet and gentle loving man

And so I shared my gift of him
With each and every one he trimmed
With all the ladies that he cared for
And that he was always there for

He held each one of you like gold
Sharing recipes of old
Weaving tales rich and wild
As he did your hair in style

I still miss him by my side
He was my life's gentle ride
What he always gave to you
Was also always mine times two

I still see the distant land
Where I first saw that sweet man
I still see those eyes so brown
How they turned my heart around

He was my soft place to land
That sweet and gentle loving man

Jack's face, normally robust and full, began to show the strain cancer caused, and it became almost skeletal. Fortunately, drugs later helped him regain some of his body mass, and his face filled out.

The picture everyone carried of Jack had been altered: once energetic and stirring, he was now weak, and often restricted to his bed. Recovery required that he spend the next seven weeks at the hospital undergoing chemo- and radiation therapy and rehab. It was not an easy seven weeks. He had to regain all the strength he'd gotten back before the stroke, and then some.

Jack had to relearn the simplest tasks, everyday functions, and movements once second nature to him: how to roll from one side to the other; how to push himself up from a lying position; how to rotate his body so he could correctly plant his feet before standing. He had to relearn everything without being able to see what he was doing.

Jack's stroke thrust him into depending on me to maintain his personal care, so every need or want fell as my responsibility to fulfill. Jack's every *movement* and *desire* required that I interact with him, grant him my full attention, and put forth every ounce of my energy. Although he had a remarkably positive attitude and a strong resolve to move forward, the effects of his blindness became close to unbearable for me.

Here's an abbreviated list of what caring for Jack entailed. I'm sure these items appear on most caregivers' lists:

Showering: At first Jack could help shower and dry himself, but months later, when the strength in his left side completely disappeared, I did it all for him. In March 2005, because I knew there was going to be a time when I would need to wheel Jack in and out of the bathroom, I had a wall around the toilet in our master bathroom removed, I expanded the shower, and removed the step up to get into it. I've never undertaken a home improvement project as valuable as this one.

Drying his hair: Jack blow-dried his hair himself, and he continued to dry it after he had a butch haircut. When he became bedridden, I towel dried it for him, and, by the time he became totally dependent on me to fix his gorgeous hair, I no longer had to worry about doing it perfectly.

Dressing: Jack now focused more on how to put his shirt on and button it correctly than on the way it looked on him. Because I had become his eyes, he relied on me to tell him these things.

Brushing his teeth: Up until his last week of life, Jack was usually capable of doing this for himself.

Shaving: I shaved Jack. It remains in my memory as one of my sweetest and kindest chores. I truly enjoyed touching his beautiful face this way; it provided me with comfort.

Using the toilet: At first we walked hand in hand to the bathroom; eventually, he had to transfer to a roller seat, and I wheeled him to the toilet. When Jack became immobile, but not bedridden, and needed only to urinate, I no longer moved him to the bathroom every time he had to "go"—which was often. Jack had always been one to frequently urinate, and this didn't change when he became ill. On these occasions, he cried out his need to go, and I responded by helping him use a urinal.

Eating: I witnessed every bite of food Jack took in. At first he was capable of at least attempting the voyage from plate to lips, but this eventually gave way to me feeding him. Like shaving, this provided me with deep comfort.

Some tasks became more frustrating (exhausting) for me than others. For example, when Jack wanted a drink, he asked for his beverage of choice, and I brought it to him. And that was fine. But then he asked for more to drink, and I brought it. Then he asked, and I brought, and he asked, and I ... .

In a frantic attempt to lessen Jack's requests for "something to drink," thus my trips to the kitchen, I devised a drinking fountain for him: a cooler filled with ice with three large plastic cups inside, placed next to his chair. I ran plastic tubing from the cups to a clasp on his lapel. Now all he had to do was find the plastic tubing, select his drink—water or soda— and sip away.

My ingenious device worked fairly well; however, when the tubing became unclipped from Jack's lapel, or a cup went dry, I had to take care of it. Also, Jack just plain disliked my setup (he was demanding before his illness), but in order to alleviate at least a small amount of running, I forced him to use it.

Jack's care required a lot of work from me, but I was willing to do it because I desperately wanted to keep him at home. I couldn't bear the thought of placing him in a nursing home or any other care facility; that would have been physically, emotionally, and financially disastrous for us. I successfully kept him in our home, and I remain grateful to this day that he never had to face the indignity of being a resident in a care facility.

As much as I wanted Jack at home, and as often as I tried to remain positive, and despite my best intentions, caring for him wore me out—wore us *both* out. Our journey became a living hell, one that cannot be fully comprehended unless you've taken it yourself. My pendulum began to consistently swing between frustration and exhaustion.

One day, when I was particularly irritated with Jack because he resisted following my requests, he snapped at me, "You just try putting blinders on, and see how difficult this is to do." I must have been giving him directions his brain wasn't able to correctly forward to his body.

If you put on blinders, you realize the magnitude of loss of sight. If you lay a lead weight over one side of your body, you require considerable concentration and effort to move, if you can move at all. Add cortical blindness to the equation, and you have an impossible situation.

Once Again See Me

I knew I saw you resting there all cuddled up and warm
I knew you were in blankets seeking comfort from the storm
I knew you called my name and I answered each request
I knew my patience was not always quite the best

I knew that overall I tried to be there for your call
I knew and hoped that somehow I could change just what I saw
I knew what you did and how you tried to stay the course
I knew and marveled at your patience, iron will and force

But the only hope I had was one that would not be
For your brown eyes to open up and once again see me

I knew you put your fork in hand and moved it toward your face
I knew it sometimes missed its mark but you did it all with grace
I knew I could not change one single thing that you endured
I knew regardless of my wish there would not be a cure

I knew you struggled daily seeing only darkened space
I knew you tried to place your cup back in its proper place
I knew I could not help you see the colors in your life
I knew regardless of my hope you'd see just afterlife

The only hope I had was one that would not be
For your brown eyes to open up and once again see me

I knew our walks together would last just a short time more
I knew that cancer's deadly march was destined for your door
I knew the visions that you saw were real just to you
I knew the visions of me here without you were true too

I knew you could not see me as you drew your final breath
I knew yours were just images of memories in your head
I knew I could not help you see the colors in your life
I knew regardless of my hope you'd see just afterlife

I know my hardest memory was the one that found you blind
I know I could not change it all regardless of the time
I know I could not help you see the colors in your life
I know regardless of my hope you'd see just afterlife

The only hope I had was one that is to be
Now your brown eyes open wide and once again see me

Jack loved Wintergreen Lifesavers; he called them "Winto Greens." When he desired a piece of candy to sweeten the day, he simply called out "Winto Green!" and I came running. Needless to say, I was not always happy to hear those words, and I often became annoyed. *How many times a day does he have to ask? How many Lifesavers can one man eat?*

Today, I would give anything to hear him ask for a "Winto Green" one more time.

> "Beauty that dies the soonest has the longest life. Because it cannot keep itself for a day, we keep it forever. Because it can have existence only in memory, we give it immortality there."
>
> Bertha Damon

4.

Frustration: A Good Man's Heart

Christmas 2004 marked Jack's release from the hospital to a life filled with darkness, his physical appearance altered by more than a new haircut: a baseball-sized portion of his right skull, which had become infected, had been removed during a third surgery. This Christmas also found us without our dear friend and companion of 15 ½ years, Dusky.

The previous June, Dusky had fallen ill and nearly died. At that time, we were close to having him put to sleep, but we chose to wait. Jack and I wept and talked about the eventual death of our friend. (Little did we know what other deaths lay in store for us.) When Jack was admitted to the hospital for his first surgery, Tom took Dusky home to live with him and his family, and he stayed there during Jack's rehabilitation.

Jack and Dusky were able to spend a few hours together when Jack was granted a 3-hour Thanksgiving release from the hospital. This was the last time Jack petted Dusky. He was in St. Joseph's ICU recovering from his stroke and coma when Dusky's condition worsened, and I decided it was time I had Dusky put to sleep.

On the morning of December 6, I said good-bye to Dusky, and a few hours later I entered Jack's room, took his hand, and said, "Good morning," in as cheery a voice as I could muster.

"John, what's wrong?" Jack asked. "Your hand is freezing." (His tactile sense became keener after he lost his sight.)

"Dusky just died. I took him to the vet to be put to sleep."

"Oh, dear, dear Dusky."

We held one another and cried.

It was around this time I mentioned to a friend that I felt like I was beginning to lose everything I loved, that I couldn't escape the steady drone of the death march enveloping me. These were prophetic words that became more true as time passed. I couldn't have imagined it. Even now, there are times I can't fathom the great amount of loss that occurred in only a few months.

We were determined to adjust to Jack's blindness, to make the most of life, so we investigated what it would take to get a Seeing Eye dog, and several times we went to the Arizona Council for the Blind for suggestions and assistance. The Council's goal was to help him become more independent, an admirable goal, I thought. They attempted to teach him how to use the public bus system, but Jack told me they were wasting their time. "I'll never use them [buses]. If I want to go anyplace, you will be taking me."

I guessed he was right, but I was grasping at straws, hoping he would improve and would someday need to ride a bus, that he had more time to live. Yet, even if Jack had wanted to ride buses, he might not have been able to: his situation was complicated by delusions, caused by either cortical blindness or his brain tumor. (In January we learned his brain tumor was back.)

Frustration—Emotion associated with being prevented from accomplishing a purpose or fulfilling a desire; feelings of discouragement.

Brain tumor patients have delusions; they believe things are happening that really aren't. This is a normal and anticipated side effect of the tumor. Doctors use it as a means to monitor the progression of the disease.

People with cortical blindness also experience delusions; they think they can see when what's there is in their mind's eye. They respond to what they see, and, to those around them, it appears as if they are delusional.

Jack's cortical blindness, combined with his delusions, created a scenario that had his doctors mystified. I frequently and desperately sought information from them that would help me differentiate between delusions caused by his blindness and those caused by his tumor. I grilled them. "Tell me, how do I know when is he having a delusion associated with his brain tumor, and when is it due to his cortical blindness?" They had no answers. If the medical community didn't have the answers, what was I supposed to do? Doctors had failed us once again.

Living with Jack's delusions was exasperating. For example, one morning I awoke to find him walking out the bedroom door and into the short hallway leading to the kitchen.

"Stop!" I screamed. "What are you doing?"

"I'm just going to the kitchen."

"Oh, for Christ sake! Get back here!" I yelled, then ran to him, and escorted him back to bed. If he fell again, who knew what could happen to him? I couldn't risk finding out. Jack didn't realize he required total assistance to walk from point A to point B. The brain tumor and cortical blindness had worked together to erase his mapping capability, so he couldn't rely on his memory to tell him the layout of the house, or what it looked like. He didn't know where the chairs or the tables were, where anything used to be. His illness stole it all.

While in the hospital, Jack would try to walk around, so, to keep him from hurting himself, the staff put a vest on him, then tied the vest to his bed. He could still move, but he couldn't get up. I thought this was undignified treatment, especially for someone who only weeks prior to this had been active and independent. I vowed I would never tie Jack to his bed, and I kept my vow.

At night I tried to anticipate when Jack might decide to get up and walk around, and I kept myself awake as long as possible, but sometimes I'd conk out—I couldn't help it—only to wake up to see him standing in front of his dresser or starting to walk out of the room. Other times, I found him sitting on the edge of the bed, readying himself to stand up and walk.

"Jack, it's night," I'd say. "Lie back down."
"I want to sit on the edge of the bed."
"It's the middle of the night. Lie down."
"*You* lie down."
"Jack!"
"Leave me alone!"
I'd pull Jack back into a lying position, but he'd

push himself back up, and I'd pull him back down, and he'd push himself back up, and ... and ... this went on into the night.

"What's the big deal?" Jack sometimes asked. "I'm just sitting here."

The big deal? The deal is you falling, hitting your head, having another stroke, and who knows what else. That's the big deal!

About this time, my thoughts would return to his ill-timed and unnecessary release from the emergency room. If he'd stayed there, perhaps his blindness could have been avoided, and I wouldn't be an expert on cortical blindness and its ramifications.

Once again, I'd become angry at the hospital and its less-than-stellar emergency room evaluation of Jack. (I could have sued the hospital for at least $50,000, under the Emergency Medical Treatment and Action Labor Act, which states a hospital emergency room may not release patients in worse condition than they were admitted. But being gay, with no legal rights because I wasn't Jack's next of kin, I knew a lawsuit would have meant a lot of work without a financial payoff.)

So it was a *huge* problem when Jack left our bed. But, as I said, I was not going to tie him in. I was *not*. Instead, I leaned three dining room chairs against his side of the bed. That way, if I didn't hear him sit up, I'd at least hear him bumping into the chairs. I had to do this; after all, there was only one of me to go around.

One night I became aggravated by Jack's delusions, so I went into another bedroom to sleep—if you could call it sleep. My "rest" was fitful, interrupted by my constant trips to our bedroom to check up on Jack, who had begun to scream.

After hours of sleeplessness, I needed to find sanity in an insane situation, so I e-mailed a friend, writing: *I'm going out of my mind with the endless nights of sleeplessness followed by days of chores. I'm tired and near the point of total exhaustion.* While I typed, Jack repeatedly screamed at the top of his lungs, "Help me! Help me!"

I looked in on him several more times, but I couldn't quiet him, so I stomped outside and stood by the pool, and listened for Jack's screams, wondering if our neighbors could hear them. Who knows, they might have believed he was in terrible trouble, when, in fact, his behavior was a heightened example of what I experienced most evenings.

The pool filters and waterfall were running, muffling Jack, but once off, "Help me!" rang out loud and clear. I ran inside and again tried to calm him, but he kept insisting, "We're in a hotel in Colorado, and no one will help us." I was beside myself, trying to convince him we were at home. "Jack, stop it! You're safe in your bed!"

Finally, morning drew near, and Jack quieted, but then he complained that he had a steel plate in his head. I noticed he had scooted himself up to the top of the bed, and his head was pressing against a metal bar in the headboard. *No wonder,* I thought. I gently slid Jack away from the headboard, and we began our day the way we began many of our days: exhausted.

Months later, I hated myself for raising my voice to Jack. *How could I do that to My Banana Bread Man, the man I loved, who was blind and dying?*

But time has softened this harsh view of myself. It helped when I weighed my reactions against the torturous task of taking care of a person who had a brain tumor and was the love of my life. I was sleep deprived and emotionally exhausted. I occasionally wonder how I was ever able to pass a civil word to anyone. Yet, in spite of all we were going through, Jack's and my life moved forward. We laughed and we ... fought.

We had always been pretty much like Fred and Ethel from "I Love Lucy"—quick with the remarks, but always smothered in love—and we continued to be, and our terms of endearment, "Jackie O" and "John Boy," echoed from room to room, just as they had before Jack got sick.

And we found humor, even in delusions. I recall one afternoon, I'd realized I'd run low on Jack's medication, Ativan, prescribed during his second hospital stay to control anxiety and agitation, common side effects from brain tumors. I was irritated that I had to go to the pharmacy, and Jack must have sensed this, because he said, "You don't have to worry about getting low on that pill. We have all kinds of it."

"No, we're almost out," I said.

"If that's the case, don't worry. We have all kinds of it in the yard. It's in the rock out front. Just go chip some off and bring it in."

Well, we had a good laugh over this. And from that time forward, whenever I was low on Ativan, I said I could always get more outside, and Jack smiled. "That's right."

Occasionally, Jack saw men sitting on fences talking to each other ... in our living room, or old men standing at opposite ends of our bedroom, or a bathroom with silver pipes, which happened to be in our living room. Three weeks before he died, he was totally bedridden, but he told his visitors he had walked down the street to pick up the mail, and that he'd gone for a walk earlier that morning.

Sometimes his delusions were too much for me to emotionally take; other times, I used them as an opportunity to discuss what he was seeing, and, in a way, incorporate what he saw into the journey. When this happened, some of the pain caused by the delusions fell away and were replaced by a smile and a loving touch. Jack hadn't lost his hearing or sense of touch, so we concentrated on what he had, as opposed to what he didn't.

Another delightful delusional exchange occurred a few weeks before Jack's death. I was standing at his side when he suddenly gazed up at me and asked, "Who is that lady behind you in the blue dress?"

I gently said, "There's no one behind me."

"Of course there is. At first I thought it was you in drag."

I chuckled. "Nope, that wasn't me."

"Well, she has blonde hair, and it is fixed just beautifully. I must have done it for her."

Jack knew he was experiencing a delusion, but he joked, trying to make me smile. And the pendulum kept swinging.

A Good Man's Heart

Your passion was great; your spirit was so bright
In me a shattered man exists, a sad and lonely
*   sight*

The choice to take you first, me, a crying soul
Makes no sense at all to me, in you a treasure told

A cold reality of death now stares me in the face
Is there a good man left in here to keep me in this race?

I'd gladly take the path that sent you to this early grave
And die your death a million times so all could see you saved
Where is the justice in a plan that grabs a man so fine?
And leaves on earth a soul like mine wilted on the vine

How can my life continue now with you simply not here?
A good man who had kept me strong has vanished into thin air
In you a good man did exist some heritage to pass
In me, a passage is not there no reason here to grasp

A cold reality of death now stares me in the face
Is there a good man left in here to keep me in this race?

Your family has been torn apart by cancer's deadly leech
The son that you loved more than life is way beyond my reach
A good man's love did keep him here but mine could not compare

Your illness and your death would send him back to some nowhere

Granddaughters that do share your name are now seldom around
And will be swept away for good when moving vans leave town
The life we shared together was so easily untwined
The family that was solid could not stand the test of time

A cold reality of death now stares me in the face
Is there a good man left in here to keep me in this race?

A father who was just like you is yours to see each day
The best of what your family was now spirits far away
The good man who inspired you is with you by your side
The good man who inspired me has left me here to cry

A cold reality of death now stares me in the face
Is there a good man left in here to keep me in this race?

The question that I asked to start—how can this life go on?
Is answered in the life you led and speaks now from beyond
The good man who inspired me is also by my side

*A good man's heart beats in me, from this I shall
not hide*

*A cold reality of death may stare me in the face
I found in me a good man's heart to keep me in the
race*

Despite Jack's delusions, he was still in tune with his surroundings, and he had a clear sense of self. He remained cognizant every moment of this ordeal. He would look directly at me after telling me about something he was seeing and calmly say, "I suppose you're going to tell me that what I'm seeing is not really there." What he saw in his mind's eye wasn't real, but his grasp of the needs of the individuals around him, his continued normal and customary interactions with friends and family, and his ability to be humorous remained as strong as ever. His surgeon would attest to that.

Once, after Jack was wheeled into the operating room, he said to Dr. Nakaji, "I see you're going to take another stab at it." And then, when it was time for *another* surgery, Jack was again true to form. He said, "Well? How many times do you have to do this before you get it right?"

Jack's humor wasn't lost on Dr. Nakaji, but some of our friends, family members, and customers couldn't see it. They missed the fact that he was completely present. They could hear only the delusions being played out in front of them, or see the physical changes in Jack. They failed to look for what was still there.

People feared what they would see when they visited their dear friend, so they avoided him, failing to grasp that he was still the same person. Although many people continued to visit Jack, far too many backed away.

Yes, he looked different, but he was unaware of what he looked like to others; the only change he was conscious of was that he was blind. His delusions were real to him, therefore, they did not represent anything unusual. He still greeted each visitor with a smile and a hug; moreover, in his mind, he could still walk; all anyone had to do was talk with him, and they'd see Jack as he always was: a man with a quick wit and a remarkable sense of humor.

Frequently the ill and disabled are overlooked, looked past, or through, by people who don't appreciate the beauty that still remains. By failing to partake in and witness Jack's illness, many people lost out on an amazing opportunity to experience the extraordinary individual he was, because his true essence became the most apparent in the closing days of his life.

As difficult as his illness was for me, I am grateful I did not miss one day, one instant, or one heartache of it. Witnessing and directly participating in this process was what later allowed me to heal.

Most mornings I asked Jack, "What can you see today?"

Often, he would say everything was the same as usual, or "Shades of gray."

Then one morning I asked, "Can you see me?"

Jack smiled.

"Yes, you can," I teased. "What am I wearing?"

His answer? "I don't know, but you're beautiful."

"Normal day, let me be aware of the treasure you are. Let me learn from you, love you, savor you, bless you before you depart. Let me not pass you by in quest of some rare and perfect tomorrow. Let me hold you while I may, for it will not always be so. One day I shall dig my nails into the earth, or bury my face in the pillow, or stretch myself taut, or raise my hands to the sky, and want, more than all the world, your return."

Mary Jean Irion

5.

Guilt: Crazy with Watching You Slip Away

Jack bit me three times. And each time I reacted with anger. "That's it! I've had enough! Let's see how much you like biting people when you're stuck in a nursing home!"

I can't recall Jack having much of a response to my threats, and if he reacted negatively, I must have blocked it from my memory in an effort to forget these painful episodes, the final, and most painful one, occurring two weeks prior to his death.

Jack had begun to refuse to swallow his pills; he chewed them instead. Of course, this frustrated me. "What's so hard about doing what I'm telling you to do? You're supposed to swallow, not chew, the damn pills." When he still refused to swallow, I pried open his mouth and put the pills in. "Now swallow!" I ordered. Jack nipped my index finger, and I patted his cheek and firmly said, "Do not bite me." Upset and stretched to the breaking point, I asked one of Jack's visitors to take over for me, then I darted from the room.

Guilt—The fact of being responsible for an offense or wrongdoing. Remorseful awareness of having done something wrong.

As a couple, Jack and I continued to fight, however, our fights became specific to Jack's care and his stubborn insistence on doing things his way. There were fights caused by Jack sitting on the edge of the bed in the middle of the night, of course, but there were others.

As his ability to walk faded, followed by his ability to take one step, the only way I could move him from one place to another was to ask him to stand so I could stand in front of him, put my right knee between his legs, my hands on his shoulder blades, then quickly pivot and lower him into a chair on wheels. Jack fought my requests to stand. Then he fought the pivot, sitting down, and whatever else I needed him to do. Our struggles seemed endless.

As I look back on this, as a "person with 20/20 vision or as a Monday Morning Quarterback," I see that his tumor and cortical blindness were responsible for much of what I interpreted as stubbornness. If I said, "Stand up so I can turn you," I might as well have said, "Stand up so I can throw you on the floor." His tumor was taking away his ability to differentiate his right from left, the command to stand from sit, up from down. I felt horrible for screaming at him when he couldn't help himself. What I perceived as obstinacy was the nightmarish workings of his illness; it was slowly robbing him of his ability to understand simple instructions.

About swallowing pills: I eventually realized Jack didn't want to disregard my instructions. His brain was giving him mixed up feedback; it told him he was swallowing, when he was chewing. This was a sign his disease was progressing towards its final phase. In the end, his confused brain told his body, "Don't breathe" when it meant to say, "Breathe."

After he physically left me, and before that, grief would constantly whisper reminders to me about my words spoken to Jack in haste: "Sit down!" "Stand up!" "Don't pee now; you're on the carpet." "Jack, *look* at what you did." "Oh, what a mess." "Where are you going?" "Don't move!" "I just brought you to the bathroom, and you have to go back again?" "Why is this happening to us?" "Why is this happening to you?" "When will this nightmare end?" God help us." "God help me." "God!"

These harsh words haunted me, even though I recognized I did the best I could under our desperate circumstances. I had to forgive myself many times, and I apologized repeatedly to Jack for my shortcomings and my inability to handle the deterioration I was witnessing. I would lay my head on his lap and cry. I'd say, "Jackie O, I'm sorry for screaming at you." Jack always patted my head and gently said, "That's okay. I'm sorry, too."

My guilt continued to plague me, even after Jack died, so I began to write letters to him. In one letter, dated October 14, 2005, I spoke to him about how badly I behaved toward him:

> Dear Jack,
> There were times when I would become furious when I was cleaning you, or when you would not follow my instructions to stand. I know we seemed to start almost every day with a verbal struggle, until you became bedridden. I should have known better—but I did not—and I feel bad about this. I know I apologized

almost every time I did this. Please know how very sorry I am for this shortcoming.

I should have spent more time just sitting with you—when you were in the living room (and could walk) and then when you were bed-ridden. Sometimes you just wanted to sit and talk; sometimes I did that and other times I did not. The only excuse I have is that I needed to try to keep busy doing other things; I was almost crazy with watching you slip away from me. Now I wish I had just sat there and been with you all the time, but I also know that caregivers need to pull away sometimes. Despite knowing that, I still feel bad for not spending more time with you.

Love, John Boy

I became a person I didn't recognize, a person Jack didn't recognize. *He* was supposed to be the caretaker in our relationship, the one who fussed and fumed about getting everything done, the nester who took care of me. And I became angry and bitter that the man I loved, who used to be independent and in charge, was now dependent on *me*. Our roles had flipped. It's difficult to be expected to give when you're used to receiving, likewise, it's a chore to receive when you're used to giving. This meant we struggled to adapt to our obligatory new positions in our relationship.

One day I told him, "I really miss being taking care of by you."

He replied, "That was one of the nicest things you have ever said to me."

Acts of forgiveness became as much of a ritual for

us as eating three meals a day. I forgave Jack, and he easily forgave me, but I would eventually have to struggle through the major task of self-forgiveness, as that was going to be the only way to make peace with these issues.

Over time I forgave myself and accepted that I did the best I could, under the catastrophic circumstances I faced. I reminded myself that, because of me, he never had to experience the indignity of being assigned a room in a nursing facility. He was cared for at home, his home, the home he loved, that we built together.

As I worked through my guilt I came to realize the positive tasks I performed for Jack far outweighed the negative things I did, what I perceived as my shortcomings. I was also able to absolve myself because he would have been the first one to absolve me. Eventually I was able to banish all guilt and regret that remained after his death.

Yes, I got frustrated and I lost my temper and, as I said, Jack consistently forgave me. But after he died, I continued to wish I'd behaved more compassionately. Yet, it's fair to say, he wasn't always compassionate with me, especially when he knew I was exhausted. He was often demanding. Pushy even. (He was this way before he became ill.) And he could run me ragged with his commands.

One of my most vivid memories of the hubbub of demands that could surround Jack takes place in May 2005. Judi, our friend from Michigan, had flown to Arizona to help care for Jack. She stayed for 12 days! (No other friend or family member provided this many consecutive days of hands-on, indepth care. This was a true act of love.) Judi and I shuttled Jack out to the backyard so he could soak up a little sunshine and we could muster a few moments of rest.

But we were outside fewer than five minutes when the demands started flying: "Could you get me a glass of water?" "Could I have a Winto Green?" "I have to go to the bathroom." "Could you pop some popcorn?" "My water glass is empty." "Where's that Winto Green?" "I have to go to the bathroom." "Is there more popcorn?" "Could I have a 'tooth picker'?" "I'm hungry." "What is there to eat?" "I can't find the phone." "Dial Brenda's number for me." "I have to go to the bathroom." "Could I have a comb?" "I need my brush." "I'm thirsty." "I'm hungry." "I have to go to the bathroom." "I'd like another glass of water."

Requests came in such rapid succession that neither Judi nor I could relax. We finally worked out a system: We'd each take on two requests at a time; that way the other person could catch their breath. It is a good thing we did this, because Jack's nonstop requests went on for an hour and a half. Exhausted, we wheeled him back inside, then we took turns napping.

It wasn't always this difficult to care for Jack. For example, between his second and third hospital stay, he and I had an especially loving seven weeks at home together. But then on January 29, 2005, he had to return to the hospital for another surgery, his fifth. His first surgery, on October 5, 2004, was to remove "all that they could see" of a brain tumor; the second, to run a shunt from the right side of his brain; then that became infected, so he had a third surgery, to run a shunt from his brain down his left side and into his abdomen.

He then had a fourth surgery to remove a portion of the right side of his skull because it, too, had become infected. (Given only a one-percent chance of infection, Jack was unlucky enough to be stricken by it twice; it was like winning the lottery in reverse. I began to wonder if he could survive hospital stays, much less his deadly disease.)

Each surgery was successful, and his immediate problems were resolved, however, the surgeries also removed some of his abilities. Most of his strength could be regained through rehabilitation, but other abilities were permanently gone.

On Saturday evening, January 29, 2005, I walked into our bedroom to help Jack get ready for bed, but instead of covering him with blankets and kissing him goodnight, I had to watch in horror as he had a seizure. It didn't last long, but it was frightening to watch; I can only imagine how Jack must have felt when those pulses were going through his body while he was unable to see what was going on. Once again, cancer's cruelty was evident.

As the ambulance sped away with Jack, My Banana Bread Man, I thought, *I had him. I lost him. I found him again. Now he's slipping away from me once more.*

Jack spent the next six weeks in the hospital, and while he was there, I continued to be his advocate and gatekeeper; I knew I had to constantly guard against his receiving poor care. It didn't concern me if the hospital was short on staff, or if it had a cumbersome bureaucracy; all I knew was he was going to be safe and cared for.

Being his advocate required vigilance. I couldn't let up, couldn't turn away for a minute. I don't know how many times I had to point out to the staff that Jack could not see. What was obvious to me was, much to my dismay, overlooked by them. They were supposed to help him take his medication, but pills often got lost in his bed sheets or dropped on the floor.

Again and again, I had to tell them to change Jack's soiled linens. They didn't seem to comprehend that he couldn't see the Call button, so he couldn't ask for help. So he soiled his bed. Then they had the audacity to scold him ... for their mistake. When Jack told me what had happened, I became livid. "How could he help it?" I said. "How dare you scold a blind man! Who has a brain tumor! Who can't feel his left side!"

After one of these instances, it dawned on me that Jack was just a number to them, a body assigned to bed A or B, in room number such-and-such. I became determined to change their perceptions of him. I had to make him real, a person with a past. If I had to "get in their face" to show them that Jack was a human being, a man who had been strong and vibrant only a few months earlier, that he was not just a face, in a bed, in a room, then I would.

I taped photographs of Jack to his door. I included shots from our vacations and other times when he was strong and healthy and "sighted." I also posted a letter, requesting that staff keep in mind that Jack had a past and people who love him, people who will be watching out for him:

Dear Hospital Staff,

These pictures are of the man you are caring for in this hospital bed. They are recent pictures. He was a vibrant, healthy, warm, kind and caring man on 10-2-04. Although not physically healthy now he is still all these things to those who love him. He may not look the same to you, lying in this bed, but the only things that have changed are his health and the way he physically looks. He has lived a beautiful life surrounded by many friends and family. Jack was a well-known and talented hairdresser who owned and operated a successful beauty salon in Fountain Hills, Arizona, for nearly twenty years. He is much more than "just a patient" who occupies this hospital room, its number listed outside his door.

He is the most important person in my life, and how he is cared for is extremely important to me and many people who love him—family, friends, and former customers. We have been partnered for more than 26 years, probably longer than many of you who care for him have been alive. How he is cared for during the times I am not here is as important to me as how he is cared for when I am here.

I ask many questions about his care. Please be prepared to answer any questions and concerns I may raise about Jack's care.

Please care for him as if he were the most important person in your life.

Thank you,

                         Jack's Partner, John

This simple action profoundly impacted how staff interacted with Jack from then on. He must not have been the only one who had lost his ability to see, because my providing pictures and a history of the man who occupied that bed in that room, opened their eyes.

Jack went through two weeks of surgical procedures, then four weeks of rehabilitation—another long and emotional six-week stretch. Then on March 12, three days before he was to be released, he had to have surgery to solidify a disc in his spine. He had broken his back, but I never determined how it happened. Either his medication to stop brain swelling had weakened his bones, causing them to break, or he was dropped by a staff member. No one knew.

Needless to say, I was relieved when he was back home with me, his care in my hands. Jack was safe at home, away from the cold hospital atmosphere and bureaucracy and the inevitable death that resides in medical institutions.

On March 15 we returned home as a couple for the last time. We were about to complete a journey that had started 27 years earlier. The ending would not be easy for me, for Tom, and, especially, not for Jack. We were about to face the hardest time of our lives, but Jack continued to surprise us: he left the hospital already functioning at 90 to 95 percent of his pre-seizure capacity. I considered this to be amazing, since he was totally blind—and well aware that death was looming.

Given these handicaps, other people might not have had the stamina to go on. I was blessed to be able to watch Jack use his inner strength, to be next to him as he faced his death.

"When it is dark enough you can see the stars."

Charles A. Beard

6.

Despair: Anchor Lost, Spirit Broken

Jack and I were partnered nearly three decades, spending almost every day together since we met. From the beginning our families loved and accepted us, which we knew was a true blessing. We never saw the need to have a commitment ceremony—we didn't exchange rings until we'd already been devoted to each other for 20 years—because we didn't require the trappings that would force or legally obligate us to be together. Yet, we were as married and committed as any heterosexual couple, our lives and finances totally intertwined. (Our wills stated that the surviving mate was to inherit everything.) Both Jack and I were fathers to Tom.

When Jack's illness unfolded, Tom was 35 years old, and he and his wife Karrin were exceptionally supportive through the first seven months of our ordeal (through early May). But after this, Jack's physical deterioration sped up, and it became increasingly apparent that Tom was having a difficult time dealing with it. His regular visits became shortened, then sporadic, and then, when he did visit, rather than sit with his father, he cleaned our kitchen or chatted with visitors.

Of course, Jack noticed this, and in late May, he

said to me, "My own son can't stand to look at me." His pain broke my heart.

Despair—To be overcome by a sense of futility or defeat. Utter lack of hope.

I had already known Tom almost as long as I'd known Jack, having been introduced to him only days after Jack and I'd gotten together. Even though Tom's mother had custody of him, he was still close to his dad, and he repeatedly visited us, or his paternal grandmother, in Norway. After we moved to Arizona, he and Jack remained close, so close, that Tom moved to Arizona in the summer of 1992. It was a joyful day when he pulled into our driveway, his car loaded with his belongings!

Tom graduated from high school in 1987, then served two years in the Army. After that he enrolled in college, and participated in what many college freshmen did: a lot of partying and a little bit of studying. When Jack got wind of Tom's antics, he told him, "I'm not going to pay for college so you can party. Here's the deal: you finance your own education with school loans, and when you graduate, I'll pay them off for you." This was Jack's way of encouraging Tom to invest in his education. Tom had other plans, though, and he later dropped out of school. (Of course, being Jack's son, he went on to be successfully employed.)

I was always made to feel close to Tom, like I was a "real" father, and I loved him as if he were my "real" son. Many times I was Tom's "point man" with Jack. He often relied on me to do "verbal leg work" on his behalf.

He would bounce ideas off me before taking them

to Jack, as I tended to be a good shock absorber for their relationship; I could smooth out some of the bumps that resulted from Jack's high-spirited demeanor.

Jack was always physically and mentally three steps ahead of everyone else, so he often gave the impression that he was done with a conversation and had already moved on to another thought. (He had moved on, but that didn't mean he'd forgotten what was said; years later, he could recite, verbatim, the entire conversation.) If you dared to continue with the conversation, he'd let you know he was impatient with you, or bored with the topic.

Add Jack's crazy-flighty Lucy Ricardo attributes—a part of his joyful, fun-loving, spontaneous personality—and his tendency to completely control whatever and whomever was in his environment, and you had a complex and confusing situation. You would feel like he was saying, "We're finished with this moment. Let's get to the next one."

I'm sure Tom felt approaching me about conflicts between Jack and him would produce calmer discussions and more productive interactions than if he went to Jack right off the bat. I was glad to be able to help, as I often proved to be just the dose of "vitameatavegamin" they needed to get through their conflicts.

In 1994, Tom married Karrin, a former employee of mine. I often kidded Tom about this, telling him I knew his wife long before he did. Adding her to our family was as normal and natural as could be, because she fit in well, and we wholeheartedly welcomed her into our otherwise untraditional family, which was traditional in every sense of the word. We celebrated all holidays, birthdays, and special events together, in genuine harmony.

Tom and Karrin's union produced Madison, a wonderful granddaughter who brought indescribable joy to Jack. (She also brought me my only possibility of being a grandfather. It never mattered that we weren't blood relatives.) When Jack became ill Madison was four years and four months. At first she visited him often, but when Tom started to pull away, she saw him less and less, much to his sorrow. The knowledge that he would never see her grow up was already eating Jack up, but being denied the pleasure of her company while he was alive, compounded his sadness.

Around the eighth month of Jack's illness, our sound family unit, painstakingly developed, began to unravel. I refer to this in two lines in a poem: "The life we shared together was so easily untwined. The family that was solid could not stand the test of time." Tom was dealing with Jack's imminent death in his own way: by distancing himself. But Jack needed to see his son, and his absence became increasingly painful.

I knew I was in a no-win situation, but I felt Jack's needs were paramount, so in early June, I forced the issue with Tom, and this led to an argument. I said, "Your dad is dying. He only has a few more months to live, which means you need to be a more prominent presence in his life. Your visits are socializing in the kitchen rather than attending to your dying father. You're running from death, Tom.

"I desperately need help with caring for your father. I'm determined to get it from wherever and whomever I can. What your father desperately needs is close, personal contact with you, his son. The dying always have things to share with those they love, and your father has things to share with you. A father and son need this special time together."

I won the battle, but lost the war: Tom agreed to spend more time with Jack, but our argument had a prolonged detrimental affect on my relationship with the man I helped raise, whom I considered my son. But as painful as this became for me, I would do it all again; I loved them both too much to leave things as they were.

By June 15, 2005, the day of his 56th birthday party, Jack had become immobile, nearly bedridden, and he had lost most of the feeling in his left side. But that didn't keep him, or his throngs of fans, from enjoying a spectacular celebration in his honor. Almost everyone who cared about him was there, and we all kept our spirits up through this bittersweet occasion: we knew this was going to be Jack's last birthday.

Tom wasn't there. The Sunday prior to this, he'd whispered in Jack's ear, "I have to make a trip to Michigan in 10 days, but, before that, I have to get a rental property ready to be put up for sale. This means I won't be able to make it over for your birthday or Father's Day." Jack was disappointed, and I was dumbstruck. *Given the magnitude of what's happening, and our argument two weeks ago, how could he even think of missing these events?*

After this, my perception of Tom began to change dramatically. (I later learned there was a plan afoot. He was preparing to sell the rental property, purchase land in Michigan, and leave Arizona. Communication between Tom's family and ours had become another casualty of Jack's illness. What was previously an open dialogue between a father, a son, and me became closed and secretive.)

I gave Jack two birthday gifts. One was tangible—a bottle of Drakkar Noir cologne—the other wasn't—the discontinuation of chemotherapy. His immune system could no longer fight the annoying and uncomfortable side effects—warts, for example—of the chemotherapy, and it wasn't stopping the cancer anyway. (His condition deteriorated with each passing day.) Hospice helped me come to this conclusion. They helped me to realize that even if chemo were able to extend Jack's physical presence a few more weeks, he would most likely be comatose, or extremely uncomfortable. I couldn't permit my selfish desire for more time with him to outweigh his comfort.

I did what I did for Jack's benefit, but I am still distraught whenever I think about having to make this kind of decision on someone else's behalf, especially for someone I loved more than life itself. But I'm convinced that if Jack had been capable of making this decision for himself, he would have chosen to do what I did. I can only hope that if I'm ever terminally ill, my loved ones will take the same humane course of action for me.

Close to the end of the celebration, I read Jack's birthday cards to him. I read mine last. When I finished, all I could do was cry.

> Dear Jack,
> With much love on your birthday. For all the wonderful times you have given me in my life,

Thank You! I Love You So Much. Have a great day, and Celebrate Your Life.

All My Love,

John Boy

When the party was over, Jack said to me, "That was my best party ever."

"It was, wasn't it?" I answered.

The next day Jack had a seizure, which was what it took to shock Tom into realizing that his father was not going to be on Earth too much longer. (It's not often a seizure brings benefits.) Time, which he had previously pronounced too limited, became available, and he began to see what was important in life. He began to prioritize and face harsh realities.

Tom visited Jack on Father's Day, and on two more occasions before he left on his trip to Michigan. This was progress. Time between a father and his son was secured, and their interaction flourished. I know Jack was grateful for their moments together, and I hope Tom feels the same way.

In early July, Tom was feeding Jack when I overheard Jack say, "You're a good son." He had forgiven Tom, who was, and still is, a good son.

Three Small Words

Three small words in dreams are spoken
Three small words in dreams unbroken
Nighttime is the only breakthrough
When I hear you say "I Love You"

In the darkness these words tell me
What I lost, how they propelled me

Anchor lost, my spirit broken
Three small words in dreams are spoken

You would ask the question clear
Then the answer I would hear
"Do you know how much I love you?"
"Lots and lots" your loving coo
In these words my dreams make do
And my answer—"Love you, too"

It was not that long ago
I could see and you would show
You would tell me in a phrase
How much you loved me, in what ways

Spoken with the morning's mist
Spoken with each good-night kiss
Three small words to start the day
Three small words, we'd end that way

You would ask the question clear
Then the answer I would hear
"Do you know how much I love you?"
"Lots and lots" your loving coo
In these words my dreams make do
And my answer—"Love you, too"

Now I must depend on slumber
Close my eyes and let dreams lumber
Before I fall asleep I ponder
Will you visit me, I wonder

Will you speak these three small words
While I sleep between these worlds

In the darkness three words tell me
What I lost, how they propelled me

Even death's attempt to break us
Cannot separate what made us
I may not see and hear you say
That you love me every day

Love creates a bridge of joy
That even death cannot destroy
You may not be in my sight
But our love visits every night

In my sleep the question clear
Stated it like a fact, I hear
"Do you know how much I love you?"
"Lots and lots" your loving coo
In these words my dreams make do
And my answer—"Love you, too"

When Jack was hospitalized in early October 2004, and then again at the end of the month, family members, friends, and Jack's customers inundated our lives, but when he was hospitalized the third time, I noticed his room wasn't as crowded as it had been, and his phone not as busy. People began to stay away. I could relate to what they were feeling—having participated in every day of this struggle—and I understood their need to distance themselves from the physically visible tragedy, but *we suffered* from their absence: we needed their support. Luckily, our Angel of Mercy appeared.

Timmy was nearly 40 years old when we met him. It was December 2004, and Jack was ready to be released from the hospital for the second time. He was blind, so he needed 24-hour care, which was up to me to provide. I knew he would require more help than I could give, and this had to come from someone who Jack could feel comfortable with during his physical, mental, and emotional journey.

I had composed a full-page "help-wanted" sign and posted it at various sites frequented by people in the Phoenix gay community, and Timmy immediately stepped forward. I didn't need his services until the middle of January (Jack and I decided to take three weeks to adjust to our new life), but he insisted on visiting us several times (without benefit of pay) in December and early January. He wanted to be sure Jack would become comfortable with him and that they related to each other well, before he was needed full-time.

Timmy was precisely what we were looking for! He had a delightful sense of humor—an excellent match for Jack's quick wit—plus he was compassionate and caring, qualities I believed he possessed as a result of his own struggles. He grew up in a broken home; his mother left when he was seven; his family rejected him because of his sexual orientation; he had epilepsy; and he was a long-term HIV survivor. (Regrettably, some people, when they heard Jack was ill, assumed he had AIDS, which he didn't; he wasn't even HIV positive. Prejudice around HIV still cripples the hearts and minds of the U.S., but HIV has not been able to cripple the determination of those it has afflicted.)

Unfortunately, Timmy had firsthand experience with the pain associated with losing a partner: he'd suffered through the loss of three.

Before we met him, he'd already lived a tough life, but he kept going and giving, he found the time, strength, and energy to reach out to Jack and me during this devastating time.

Our Angel of Mercy used a gentle approach with Jack; he was especially cognizant of the fact that Jack was blind. He didn't push Jack to trust him, and he gave him as much time as he needed to decide if he wanted to entrust anyone other than me with his care.

In January, Timmy started to work for us, and soon the men bonded and became close—so close that one day, Jack, unhappy with me over one thing or another, stated, "I'm going to divorce you and marry Timmy."

Timmy's tenure was interrupted when Jack had a seizure and had to go back to the hospital, where he remained for six weeks. Again, he continually visited without benefit of pay. Because he had epilepsy, he had experienced seizures remarkably similar to what Jack experienced, so he helped us understand what had happened. By the end of March, Jack was home again, and Timmy began to provide me with three- to four-hour periods of relief. I used those breaks to recharge my battery, so I would have the mental energy to care for Jack.

Besides Timmy, five friends from Phoenix (Ron, Dave, Paul, Jerry, and Larry), and volunteers from Hospice of the Valley helped me. Three friends from Michigan (Judi and our two Davids) stayed awhile in our home. Thanks to these people—our saviors—I was able to take time away to rejuvenate my spirit, knowing Jack was well taken care of.

We had two hospice volunteers: Lorraine (one

of Jack's former customers) and Shep, who liked to bring Jack small gifts, particularly, unusual shaped toothpicks. Jack loved Shep's visits, so much so, he started to call all toothpicks "Shep pickers." (This is another delightful example of Jack's wonderful sense of humor, which he never hesitated to share with us, even in his final days.)

I have already stated that some of Jack's family members, friends, and customers began to fade from sight, but a strong core of supporters who were willing and able to visit, remained. Other supporters, who weren't able to visit, became a part of a news-hungry group I liked to call "Jack's Gallery." Because of them my e-mail list exploded.

I am eternally grateful to the people who stayed the course until Jack left this life, and to those who not only stayed the course, but who became more involved as his condition worsened. The true value of friendship blossomed before my eyes. Jack could not see their support, but I know he deeply felt every single gesture of love and friendship.

"When you are sorrowful look again in your heart, and you shall see that in truth you are weeping for that which has been your delight."

Kahil Gibran

7.

Death: Memories of Green

No one thought death would come for Jack as soon as it did, arriving the end of July, when we thought September was more likely. Hospice had been with us since April 25, a seizure on June 16 rendered Jack bedridden, and another, on June 25, looked like it would kill him. But he rallied.

Up until July 3, Tom and his daughter Madison continued to spend quality time with Jack, but after that, Jack never again had the pleasure of hearing Madison call him "Papa Jack." Tom started to visit alone. I was told Jack's illness was upsetting her, but I wasn't convinced. Every time she came to our home, she eagerly ran into Jack's room whenever he called for her.

I had an inkling it was not Madison, but Karrin, who was upset by his decline. I believe losing him was becoming too much for her: Only 17 years earlier, when she was 18, she watched her own father die. This inkling was confirmed by a close friend of mine. She was at Tom's home, talking about Jack, when Karrin's sister told her, "Please stop talking about brain tumors and Jack. It's upsetting Karrin, and she can't take it anymore."

Karrin was unwilling, or unable, to "stay the course" through the final months of Jack's illness, and it was unfortunate that her past kept Madison from seeing him. As much as I wanted to tackle this issue, though, I couldn't; I was too busy keeping the man I loved as comfortable as possible.

July passed as a blur. I spent it caring for Jack and making arrangements for a seven-day getaway in Los Angeles. I desperately needed time, a break from home, to rejuvenate; I needed a few days respite from the sorrow surrounding Jack. But before I could go I had to perform scheduling gymnastics. First, I had to find the right hospice respite care facility, and I succeeded. I told Jack he was going to a "spa," where he would receive massages, and, bless his heart, he was excited about this venture. Second, I needed to arrange visitors to cover all the hours I'd be away. I didn't want him to be left alone. I sent out this e-mail message:

> Obviously the overall situation with Jack's health is not promising, and we know that at some point the cancer will take his life; we just do not know when. It could be tomorrow; it could be later, but we know his time is slowly running out. Any future seizure or TIA could present us with the life-ending process, which we wish we could avoid, but that we know is inevitable. His seizure medication has been increased, however sooner or later it will have no affect on the process, and he will be taken from us.
>
> I realize that all these words are difficult to read—believe me they are even more difficult to write. So many of you have taken time from your lives to come and visit Jack and I cannot begin to tell you how much your gift of time has meant to him. No, he does not look like the same person you all knew, but his warm and loving personality is

A Journey Through Mourning

there for all to see, if you have the strength to visit with your friend. I will not thank those who have given Jack this gift of time—here—since you know who you are—and you will be forever changed for having spent this time with him.

Every time I leave the room, kiss him goodnight, and have any interaction with this man I have shared my life with, I realize it may be the last time he may recognize my voice or know who I am. Time is not on your side if you are delaying any interaction with Jack, so if you are contemplating involvement you would need to do it now—not later.

Once again many thanks to all of you who have sent messages of support, made phone calls, prepared food, but most of all to you who have come to visit Jack, and who would "Jack Sit" for me, and you who involved yourselves in this a most difficult journey. Soon Jack will not be here to remember what you have done for him, but I will. And your acts of kindness and involvement in this process will remain with me forever.

I received an overwhelming response to my request, and had all but a few two-hour visitor shifts covered. That arranged, I was ready for departure, but, as the day grew near, I ran into a little glitch: the hospice respite facility stated Jack would have to have had a bowel movement shortly before arriving there. I told them Jack rarely had daily bowel movements when he was well, so they needn't be concerned about it now. But they *were* concerned, and wouldn't agree to any exceptions. So over the course of two days I gave him multiple doses of stool softener, and his system accommodated the "movement police." Now we were both set to leave the next morning.

I had my bags packed and in the car before I went into Jack's room to prepare him for his ambulance ride to the "spa." But there was a problem: I couldn't wake up Jack. He seemed to be on the edge of waking, but he wouldn't do it. He had soiled himself, so I cleaned him up, and still he slept. By now, I wasn't sure I should leave him. I called hospice to ask their advice, and they insisted I take the trip. (They probably thought I was close to mental and physical collapse, and they were right.) I reluctantly agreed to go, and I sent Jack off in an ambulance.

As I was leaving town, the respite facility called to tell me he was stirring. Needless to say, I was relieved, however, when I arrived in L.A. six hours later, I learned he'd never really woken up. "Should I come right back?" I asked. No, they said; they were concerned about him, but they advised me to stay the night and then see how he was in the morning. So I stayed in L.A., but I slept fitfully ... between calls to the respite facility.

The first time I called, I couldn't believe what I heard. "I'm sorry, Mr. Davis, but we don't have your name on Mr. Orler's chart. We are not allowed to release any information if you're not named on the chart."

"What? I'm Jack's medical and legal power of attorney."

"I'm sorry, but I can't release any information. It's the law. We do this to protect the patient."

I didn't back down, and a heated argument ensued, during which I told both the staff and the nursing coordinator that if they refused to provide me my rightful information, they would meet with dire consequences. (I'd been Jack's advocate for nearly 10 months, and I wasn't going to give up that responsibility now!) Finally, I convinced them of my identity, and they told me what I needed to know.

The next morning Jack still was unconscious, possibly in a coma, an indication that the dying process might have started. *So quickly?* I thought. *I just left him yesterday. This can't be happening!*

I frantically drove back to Phoenix, giving directions to Tom over my cell phone the majority of the time. "Give him ice chips," I ordered.

"Hospice said not to give him anything," Tom said.

"I *don't care* what they said. Moisten his lips and swab his mouth."

I knew if Jack was going to wake up, he needed people interacting with him. Fortunately, I'd scheduled a steady stream of visitors. I, too, interacted with Jack; I asked Tom to hold the phone to his ear. "Wake up, Jack," I said. "I'll be there soon."

My Banana Bread Man was still unconscious when it was time for his afternoon massage, but he received it anyway. A half hour after it was completed, Tom and another visitor were sitting in Jack's room, talking about Cadillacs, when Tom commented that his dad really loved Cadillacs.

"That's right," Jack chimed in, "I've had seven."

Tom was stunned and elated. Jack had returned! And this happened about the time I made my last call before arriving at the respite facility. I was thrilled to be able to speak to my Jack.

An hour later, I entered his room to see him

slightly alert, sipping water, and eating a cookie. Jack!

As it turned out, he had been in a deep sleep. I wondered if he knew I was gone, and was *not* going to wake up until I returned. We had dodged another bullet, and I hoped we had a lot more time left, but Jack was extremely weak, and it was laborious for him to speak coherently. This told me all remnants of his "quality of life" had vanished. I knew my time with him was running short. The pendulum swung toward dreading the death of my life's partner.

On Saturday evening, July 30, I kissed Jack goodnight. "I love you," I said. Jack tried to say, "I love you, too," and that was the last time I heard his voice. He fell asleep listening to the 1971 movie "Willie Wonka & the Chocolate Factory."

Death—The act of dying; termination of life. The state of being dead. Termination or extinction.

I don't think there's a way to prepare for the loss of a loved one. When it happens, it's kind of like you're forced to give an impromptu speech. You're given no advance notice of what's expected of you, and then Bam! You're up! Bam! Jack's dead, now deal with it! You think you're ready. You know it's coming. You know what to expect—how your loved one's body will slow down, stop, change color and temperature—but only after his death will the reality crystallize for you. *He's gone*, you'll think.

On Sunday, July 31, 2005, Jack never woke up. At 3:18 p.m. he began to have a seizure, so with Timmy and our friend Pattie's assistance, I gave him two Valium enemas. When they took affect, his eyes opened wide, then closed again.

Evening's darkness arrived sooner than expected, and at precisely 6:00 p.m. there was a crack of lightning followed by a peel of thunder. Then black clouds released a torrent of rain on the Arizona desert, and Jack Orler, the finest person I have ever met, took his last breath. At his right, Tom was crying, and at his left, his lifelong partner and soul mate wept and said, "It's okay, dear Jack, you can go now. We'll be fine." Then all the love that surrounded My Banana Bread Man carried him into eternity.

Ten months of terminal illness accompanied by blindness couldn't have challenged a human's spirit any more than it did Jack's, but he went through it with simple grace and moments of contentment. His was an amazing conclusion to a remarkable life.

Memories Of Green

A killing frost fell on the ground
It took away life all around
Green and fresh what I recall
Living breathing plants so tall

Remember how the sun would shine
How the rain would feed the vines
Remember how it was all small
And how it all grew into tall

And then the killing frost arrived
With mighty force and deadly stride
It took away life all around
As dusty white fell on the ground

Death becomes what can be seen
But I have memories of green

And so it is with cancer's march
Just like the frost, a molten starch
It takes away all life around
It spreads and chokes and turns life brown

Remember how the sun would shine
How love became the storyline
Remember how we grew from small
And how we grew from small to tall

Life is like the frost we see
It sometimes kills the beauty
And underneath the killing frost
Are memories of all that's lost

Death becomes what can be seen
But I have memories of green

When frost has taken life from you
Erased and snatched what you grew
Remember how the sun would shine
How the rain would feed the vines

Death becomes what can be seen
But you have memories of green

Nothing could have prepared me for the sudden and absolute exit of Jack's physical presence from my life. Nothing! I knew he was going to die, I knew it was inevitable, but regardless of how sick he was, I always took comfort in the fact that he was still breathing. Then ... he stopped breathing, and, with shocking swiftness, his body was whisked away from me. But not before I had three more precious hours with him.

Jack lay within a gathering of loved ones, who had descended on our home when they heard the news. They sat with him, and they talked to him as if he were still alive. Numerous times I left his room, and when I returned there were declarations of love in the air. "I love you very much, Jack," many would say. "I'll miss you," others whispered. While they spoke, Jack's lips spread into a smirk and then into a full-blown smile.

Despite his lack of breath, Jack's presence was evident, and it was obvious to all of us that his smile was sending us a parting message of peace, love, happiness, and contentment. I wouldn't have expected anything less from him. The day slowly ended. It was dark when Jack was removed from our home.

I saw Jack one more time, the next day, after I'd made cremation arrangements. (I planned to have his ashes commingled with Dusky and Buck's. Buck was our cat that died in 1991. Our animals were like our children, and they will go with both of us to our final resting place.)

Tom, my mother, a few close friends, and I entered a long, brightly lit room, in which at the opposite end my Jack lay on a gurney. I walked to his side, placed my head on his chest, and cried. "You're too young to die," I said. I kissed him. I stroked his face, felt his hair. When 15 minutes had passed, I placed my index finger on his cheek and said, "I love you. I always will."

Now his presence *and* his body would be gone forever. "I saw the Master's Plan that day, right there on the floor. I saw my shadow on the ground, but his it was no more."

> *"Where you used to be, there is a hole in the world, which I find myself constantly walking around in the daytime, and falling into at night. I miss you like hell."*
> Edna St. Vincent Millay

8.

Loneliness: Empty Is Silence

When people you love are terminally ill, you wish and wish for their pain to go away. You want it all to end for them, and for you. You pray for it. You beg for it. You wonder why the god you pray to refuses to answer your prayers. Then the cold reality of death stares you in the face, and you start praying for something new. You seek the unobtainable, something you know no amount of prayer can bring you. But that doesn't stop you from wanting, from searching, from begging. That doesn't stop you from becoming lonely. Your faith is challenged, and sometimes you doubt your god exists.

You long for one more day, one more hour, one more minute. And you'd give *anything* to have it.

Finding You Who Was Here

Empty is Silence—my constant fear
Empty is Food—eaten not shared
Empty is Resting—dreams turned nightmares
Empty is Walking—paths glum and bare

Empty. Living my life without you
Empty. Crying. No trace of the you who was here
Empty. Sleeping. Finding You who was here

Empty is Silence—my constant fear
Empty is Driving—destination nowhere
Empty is Cooking—I was your taster dear
Empty is Laughing—pretending I care

Empty. Living my life without you
Empty. Crying. No trace of the you who was here
Empty. Sleeping. Finding You who was here

Empty is Silence—my constant fear
Empty is Sitting—no lap to share
Empty is Standing—next to people who stare
Empty is Removing—your clothes I now wear

Empty. Living my life without you
Empty. Crying. No trace of the you who was here
Empty. Sleeping. Finding You who was here

More than 300 people attended Jack's Celebration of Life ceremony, the Saturday after his death, in a chapel in a small mortuary overlooking the desert and the famous fountain of Fountain Hills, Arizona. (It is the largest manmade fountain in the world. You could see it from the back door of Jack's salon.) The mortuary staff had set up 225 chairs, but they were filled within minutes, which meant the rest of Jack's Gallery had to stand in the aisles, in the doorway to the chapel, and in the vestibule. Soon the parking lot was overflowing, and the surrounding streets were jammed with people approaching the chapel to celebrate a life lived well and to say good-bye to Jack.

Full are Friendships—surrounding me and caring
Full is Family—mother, father, sister here
Full of Respect—of this they all share
Full of Memories—each one beyond rare

Fully Bewildered. You are not here
Fully Engaged. Memories to share
Finding You who was here

Full are Friendships—surround me and care
Full is Family—mother, father, sister here
Full of Respect—of this they all share
Full of Memories—each one beyond rare

Fully Bewildered. You are not here
Fully Engaged. Memories to share
Finding You who was here

Full of Memories—each one beyond rare
Full of Memories—each one beyond rare
Finding in Memories. Finding You who was here

Shep approached me after the ceremony. He tried to speak but he couldn't; all he could do was hug me and cry. This beautiful man's silence said it all. He knew Jack for only a few months, but in that short time Jack greatly affected him; his death brought terrible loss. He had this effect on everyone. (This is why his death has been difficult for me to transcend.)

During the ceremony, friend after friend stood up to relate stories from Jack's magnanimous life, and, more often than not, they caused the crowd to roar in laughter. I spoke, too, about his unceasing drive to live in the moment, and how I could count on him to lift me up. (I included these thoughts in his obituary, composed three months earlier, in April, while he lay in the living room adjacent to the office. He was inching closer and closer to death, so I typed a message of love and remembrance, a tribute to My Banana Bread Man.)

Jack's Celebration of Life ceremony culminated my first 10 months of grieving. I went on to grieve for several more months. I still grieve.

Within hours of Jack's death, I suffered an additional loss: Tom and his family's presence in Arizona. They didn't leave that day, but they announced they would be gone within a year.

I was standing next to Jack's breathless body when I heard the news echo from the kitchen: "Did you know we're moving to Michigan?" Karrin said. I was blindsided! She might as well have yelled "Jack's dead! Our business here is concluded, so we're out of here!" This was one of many instances of, what I perceived to be, Karrin's poor timing and insensitivity. (Time would soften the pain of separation from Tom, but it would do little to soften the way the separation was announced.)

I'd been excluded from a family that had always boasted inclusion and communication. I didn't have any idea Tom was thinking about moving away, neither did Jack. I'll take that back: in June, I did have an inkling something was going on. Tom had purchased land in Michigan, and I asked him if he was planning to move. He brushed the idea aside—denied it—and portrayed the purchase as merely land of value near his mother's home. He said it was a good deal. I never shared this information with

Jack because, in the scheme of what was unfolding, it seemed insignificant. Little did I know, Tom's purchase was a seed that would erupt minutes after Jack's death.

Hadn't Tom repeatedly insisted he would never move back to Michigan, that it was redneck land? Yes, he had. Had Jack's death suddenly turned Arizona into a hell to run away from, and Michigan, a land of ice and snow, into heaven on earth toward which to move? What changed his mind, made him make a 180-degree turn?

If you believe those who say hearing is the final sense to leave a dying body, then you believe Jack heard "Did you know we're moving to Michigan?"

Tom had already started to withdraw from Jack in the months prior to his death, so I should have expected this escape, but I didn't, and the news crushed me. I asked, *Why? Why another loss? Isn't it enough that the love of my life just died, that Dusky died in December? Now I'm expected to live through Tom abandoning me?* Then it struck me: *I'm not the father figure for Tom that I thought I was!* This realization drove me to write the most painful lines of poetry I've ever written:

He rushes off to nowhere, to nothing, to hide
in the cold dark past of yesterday. Your spirit does not hide
A father loved so dearly. The death Tom watched was rough
The father left to guide him is not seen as good enough

*No words will stop the passage of his presence from
my space
He cannot recognize the love which stares him in
the face
No time will heal the heart and soul of someone on
the run
In you a father he did see, in me, there never was
one*

*The pain of losing you still deep, the wound so very
raw
The pending pain of losing him now sticks there in
my craw
New home, new job, new destiny. He's escaping me
and you
The son we loved so dearly is now running from
me, too*

Throughout the month of August there was a constant flow of well-wishers through, what used to be, "our" door. But as September arrived, fewer and fewer people called on me, and those who kept calling, started to do it less often. Logic told me this was normal. But this didn't stop me from sinking into loneliness, or from experiencing another death, a different kind of death—a living death. My death.

The pendulum of grief began to swing from anger to denial, fear to remorse, regret to sorrow, guilt to anxiety, and from depression to hostility. Occasionally, it swung slowly and evenly, but it usually jerked back and forth so fast that my life became a living hell, a hell I couldn't escape for six months. I greeted every day with tears.

*Loneliness—Without companions; alone.
Characterized by aloneness; solitary.
Unfrequented by people; desolate. Dejected by the awareness of being alone.*

Most people who are going through grief like mine are lucky when they have one person who can help them, someone they can confide in. I was extremely lucky: I had several outstanding confidants. I was truly blessed to be able to count on my sister Cathy, my parents, and two wonderful friends, Sharon and Judi. And there was my dear hospice counselor Ann, who also became my close friend. (There was nothing—nothing—I couldn't talk with her about.)

I was also blessed to have other genuine people like her in my life, who were willing to listen to me pour out my pain. There was Lanette, a cancer survivor who, like Jack, was diagnosed with a grade III brain tumor. (Jack's was later diagnosed as grade IV.) Hers is a wonderful story: she beat the odds—a one-percent chance of surviving two years or more with this cancer—and she has already lived eight years. She's now dedicated her life to those afflicted with this horrible disease.

There was Roy, a Canadian, who in early 2006 provided friendship and emotional counsel via a Web site. He lost his partner Paul four days after I lost Jack. Because Roy was experiencing the same kind of excruciating pain I was, he was in this dark hole with me, and he became the only soul on earth who truly understood what I was feeling.

My friend Ray, from Phoenix, also stood by me. He looked on while I struggled to come to grips with Jack and Tom's absence. (Tom wouldn't be leaving for months, but mourning had already begun.)

I started to devour all the books I could find on the subject of grief and mourning. Doing this helped me to understand what I was going through. I also began to keep a journal. I wrote and wrote and wrote some more, and soon writing became a powerful way to express my feelings, to capture my thoughts.

After a while I realized I had been recording my journey through mourning, which evolved into a tribute to My Banana Bread Man. I decided that I wanted everyone who knew and loved him to remember him. I kept thinking of the old Jewish saying: "The only truly dead are those who have been forgotten." I was determined to never allow Jack to be forgotten.

In addition to writing in my journal, I started to write poetry. (Some poems appear in this book.) And about a month after Jack's death, I began to write what I call "Letters to Jack." When a loved one dies, there's a tendency to continue to communicate in one fashion or another—we all do it.

> Dear Jack,
> I sure do miss you. I cry every day for you, but realize you will not be coming back to me. That does not stop my tears. This morning I was up by 9 a.m. and did some errands: to Eddie's to do some paperwork, then to Photo Shop to pick up the DVDs from your Celebration of Life ceremony, then to St. Vincent de Paul to return the chair that helped us out so much when you were sick.
>
> All these activities only served to be a continual reminder that you are gone and how very much I miss you. There is this huge hole

in my heart that appears un-fillable. When I was on my way home they played "MacArthur Park" (our song) on the radio, just like I did at your Celebration of Life ceremony. I cried; it never ends.

John Boy

Through Letters to Jack I shared my loneliness, guilt, and remorse:

Dear Jack,

I really miss you today. Well, I guess there is nothing new about that, but today I feel especially lonely. I don't think that human beings are supposed to live alone, and I miss sharing all our wonderful times together. We sure did have a wonderful 27 years.

I still have moments when I feel bad that I yelled at you, but I believe I am making progress in that area; the books I have read have explained so much about the heavy burden of care giving. But I still need to tell you that I am sorry for any cross word or deed directed toward you. You always forgave me, but I have felt a need to reflect on those times so that I can move properly to put them away for good. So let me say again how sorry I am for my shortcomings and also how grateful I was to be able to take care of you and keep you home throughout your illness, and that I was with you when you died—in our home—with me at your side, holding you and telling you how much I loved you. I was so glad that I was able to do that for you, and I know you would have done the same for me.

I also rehashed arguments:

Dear Jack,
I've been meaning to write to you for a few days now, as I have had something on my mind in reference to your mom and dad. I know that, many times during our relationship, when we would have an argument, I would tell you that you were "acting like Dolly" or you were "just like your mother." Thing is, sometimes I guess you were. I know that sometimes I acted like Big City Lou, and you told me that, too.

Then there were the times when you were sick and I would say those same things to you, and you would say that I did not like your mother. I really did like—even love—your mother. But I really did not like the way she treated you. It was the way she treated you that I hate, not her. You were a wonderful son who had to put up with some of the terrible verbal bashings she would hand out, especially after your father died. I know you loved her—and you were always a good son to her, always.

The real reason I wanted to write to you was to tell you that you were really much, much, much more like your father. He was a kind and gentle man, full of life, who loved everyone. You both had so many of those kind and loving personality traits. You were almost mirror images of each other. I don't know if I ever told you that directly; you may have overheard me tell others that you were very much like your father. So if I did not, I want you to know that you were indeed your Father's Son. This fact was part (a big part) of the eulogy I gave at your Celebration of Life.

I continued to write to Jack on holidays and days that were special to us, and whenever I wanted to tell him about any pain or joy that passed through my life. I wrote whenever I felt the need to share my heart and soul. In all, I wrote 20 Letters to Jack, which literally tell the story of my hours, days, and months after he died.

Soon I expanded my communication to others; I wrote countless e-mails to friends and family members, in which I shared what it was like to lose irreplaceable Jack. While doing this, I slowly began to write myself out of the depths of grief, and move closer to the "land of the living."

It has been years since Jack died, and it has been writing, more than any other activity, that has sustained me. I feel a little stronger every time I write a poem, address a fellow griever's problems, type an e-mail to friends or family members, or write a Letter to Jack. The process of using my pen to share my pain, loss, and heartache allows me to maintain an attachment to the life cruelly ripped away from me when he died.

To further my writing in those months after Jack's death, I joined GriefHealing.com, a Web site associated with Hospice of the Valley, the hospice instrumental in ensuring excellent care for Jack and hundreds of other individuals facing death. (It also provides ongoing support for surviving loved ones.)

This Web site was started by Marty Tousley, who wrote the foreword to this book. She wrote "About Grief Healing" for the Web site:

About Grief Healing

"As both a bereaved parent and child myself, I have found my own way through grief many times. As one who's always wanted and needed pets in my life, over the years I've loved, lost and mourned a number of cherished companion animals as well.

In my work as a hospice bereavement counselor, I help individuals and families understand and cope with their grief in the first year following the death of their loved ones. As a volunteer in my community, I also help adults and children who are mourning the loss of their cherished animal companions.

My years of bereavement counseling have taught me that grief is indifferent to the species of the loved one who was lost. I believe that anyone who loves greatly in life and grieves deeply in loss is deserving of whatever respect, caring and support I can offer."

GriefHealing.com was an important cog in my recovery: it facilitated my passage through mourning, and it helped me find a way to transcend grief. I used this site to converse with numerous individuals who, like me, were suffering through the loss of a loved one.

As I wrote, it soon became evident to me that everyone is affected by the deep pain associated with losing a loved one. This kind of pain is universal. I then began to look at the way society handles grief, and I wondered why it is so misunderstood. I had questions: Why do people run and hide from it? Why don't we focus light on grieving? What prevents us from openly dealing with the pain of loss? Why are we prohibited from sharing the joy that comes from remembering our loved ones?

As I continued to learn about the grieving process, I began to share what I learned online and in person, and I became a point of contact for people who were grieving. Soon my hospice counselor began to share my articles with grief groups she facilitated.

It hit me as strange that I was becoming an authority on a subject that brought me only pain, which made me cry. But I knew the only way to effectively deal with my grief was to move through it.

"Things have a terrible permanence when people die."
Joyce Kilmer

9.

Searching: Recovery Spans a Lifetime

The pendulum of grief swung madly, feverishly, the first six months after Jack's death. Seeing my torment, a few well-meaning friends offered gentle, but mistaken, guidance. "Let it go," they advised. "When you do, you'll feel better." They were kind, on the outside, but I believe they were thinking, *Enough already, John. Get over it; it's been months. All dwelling on Jack is doing is making you sad. Forget about him, and move on.*

They were ridiculing my grief! They didn't comprehend that my life had been forever changed by Jack's death. He was gone, and the man I once was went with him; all that was left was a stranger in the mirror. The man I used to be was dead, but still they expected "that" me to "move on," to get over it, to do the impossible.

Dear Jack,
Sometimes I do not know what to do with all the elements of this new life without you. Things are so foreign without you; people's reactions to me are also foreign. I am still the same person. I am still alive. I did not die, but sometimes I feel as if others think that I did.

> I am sometimes treated like the living dead, someone to be remembered but not contacted, someone to be thought of but not spoken of, someone to forget about, so that the pain will leave.
>
> John Boy

My friends' advice wasn't unique; they were repeating what society deems is the proper way to handle mourning. It says a grieving person should "let go" of their loved ones; it insists this is the only way to find closure and peace. Society is wrong! You have to keep going and allow yourself to be reborn as the new you, the man/woman who has journeyed through mourning.

I became annoyed—disgusted—by people's resistance to my grief. I received rigid and pious religious prescriptions for the correct way to handle loss, one of which was to "bury my past" and preclude Jack as a part of my future. When I refused to honor their prescriptions, I was accused of not being a man of faith.

Again and again, I defended my belief that my future was based on a remembered past, our past. I repeatedly defended my choice to rely on my deeply rooted spirituality, instead of verses in the Christian Bible.

Our disagreements put distance between us. Unable to accept my grief, they backed away. But why? Why retreat from me? Because the weight of my sorrow became too much to bear. Because I reminded them of their own sorrow. Because they were afraid, and their fear isolated me.

I Became Their Greatest Fear

Some say that I can't let go
Gentle hearts that think they know
Others say a buried past
Is where you should now rest at last

Others tell me that they know
How my past should be "let go"
How to grieve and how to cry
How to feel and when and why

Those who do not understand
Have not been to this dark land
When they could not see you here
I became their greatest fear

Friends who were the closest to us
Fussed and cared and brought food to us
Once you were no longer here
I am now what they all fear

Calls and contact used to flourish
Constant tales to encourage
Now the message is quite clear
I am now what they all fear

Those who do not understand
Have not been to this dark land
When they could not see you here
I became their greatest fear

For those who think they know it all
And those who cannot make a call

Letting go that's what I must do
But it's not you who must go

They will become my buried past
It's where they should now rest at last
Letting go that's what I must do
But it's not you who must go

Those who do not understand
Have not been to this dark land
When they could not see you here
I became their greatest fear

There's a saying that goes like this: "Grief rewrites your address book for you," and my experience confirms this. After I'd wasted too much energy responding to my critics' advice to let go, and trying to get them to see pain my way, to understand that I expected my recovery to go on forever, I finally let go ... of them. And I literally rewrote my address books. I removed names from my Christmas card and e-mail lists, keeping contact information only for family members and friends who understood the grieving process, or at least acknowledged my pain without judging me.

I also made a decision to close my ears to the chorus of misdirected advice, because if I didn't, I became so frustrated I wanted to scream, "Leave me alone! Your grief is measured in much less time than mine!"

Your Grief Is Measured In Much Less Time

For many months, I stayed connected
I shared, reached out, and felt respected
But as the months and years have faded
I know your heart is feeling weighted

He was my bright shining star
His loss, a stunning, jolting, jar

It's not that I have changed my stance
I speak of love and lost romance
I write of tears and grief that's molten
Of broken hearts and futures stolen

I talked of pain that's here and real
I made you think and made you feel
I seldom left without a passage
To lift your heart and send a message

He was my bright shining star
His loss, a stunning, jolting, jar

I have tried with so much passion
To talk and teach and show compassion
All this despite my own faith shaken
My spirit crushed, feeling forsaken

I tried to put you front and center
To help you grieve and to remember
But as the months and years have faded
I know your heart is feeling weighted

He was my bright shining star
His loss, a stunning, jolting, jar

My recovery spans a lifetime
Yours is measured in much less time
He was my bright shining star
His loss, a stunning, jolting, jar

Some of you don't want to hear
Of all the pain and all the fear
Run from all that's here and real
Run and do not think or feel

Some of you I'm gently leaving
Letting go and sadly grieving
I seldom leave without a passage
To lift your heart, so here's my message

He was my bright shining star
His loss, a stunning, jolting, jar

My recovery spans a lifetime
Yours is measured in much less time

    A few friends and family members couldn't walk the road of mourning with me, but many could, and these kind souls became the core of my support. They moved toward my grief and drew closer to me. They sustained me with phone calls, asked how I was feeling, and then listened to every word I said while I cried on their proverbial shoulder.

    They extended invitations and opportunities for me to get out, and they complimented me on my strength of character, my ability to move forward, and on my devotion to Jack's memory. They often remarked on my great capacity for fostering his legacy. I was humbled by their loving actions toward me, as well as overjoyed—and grateful beyond words—for their kindness. Because of them I could meet the challenges thrown at me.

Searching—Examining closely or thoroughly. Keenly observant.

A little voice inside me became a constant companion, reminding me I was on a journey that would take the rest of my life. It would be a slow journey, taken one baby step after another, but it was clear that forgetting Jack was not going to lessen my grief or shorten how long I'd grieve. The only way I would ever achieve *any* peace was through finding My Banana Bread Man, by remembering him. Death, in its bizarre way, was forcing me to look at my blessings.

I tried to remember as many details about Jack as I could. This comforted me, and I found it sustained my connection to him as well as maintained my emotional bond with him. My life was enriched each time I recalled these things about him:

His walk, the way his arms swung when he moved, how his feet hit the ground.

The way he talked. I catch myself using vocal inflections Jack did. It's only natural that I do that, after so many years with him. I'm pleased when friends say "You said that just like Jack would have. It was like he was here."

His special way of telling me he loved me. "Do you know how much I love you? Lots lots." Whenever I sign off on an e-mail, or letter, with the words "Love you, lots lots," I'm reminded of him.

Jack's signal that he was ready to wind up a phone conversation. He'd say "Soooo ... " I do the same thing, and I love it, because it allows him to live through me, and by remembering this, I heal.

How he followed up a request with the words "just once." He'd say, "Could you bring me a cup of coffee, just once?" It's quirky, but I'm fond of it. I don't want to ever let this go.

I don't want to let *anything* about Jack slip away from me, or from anyone who loved him. And if remembering makes me cry, so be it, because every tear I shed brings me one tear closer to feeling peace.

"When the rain washes you clean you'll know. You will know."
Stevie Nicks, "Dreams"

10.

Forgiveness: My Heart Will Have to Lead This Race

By the time 2006 arrived, I'd stumbled through five torturous months without Jack, waking up every morning bewildered, uncertain how I'd manage another day. And each month brought painful "firsts": the anniversary of our meeting, Halloween, Thanksgiving, Christmas, and New Year's Eve spent without Jack at my side.

> My Dear Jack,
> Well, I am sure lost without you today. Of course, I miss you every day and every hour of every day, but this is the first major holiday without you here. I woke up crying this morning thinking of all the good holidays of the past and how much I miss you now and wish you were here for this one too. Everyone says that these memories will someday bring me joy. Not yet. But I'm hoping.
> John Boy

I didn't decorate the house for Christmas; I didn't have it in me. Instead, I burned five candles in Jack's honor. When Christmas day arrived I wrote in a Letter to Jack: "I made it through the first one, this

Christmas without you. The son we loved so dearly is now running from me, too."

At this time, I was trying to find a way to forgive others for abandoning me. I perceived abandonment as something as simple as a friend not understanding the value of "remembering" Jack, or as complicated as Tom and his family driving away from me, their possessions packed in a moving van.

My Heart Will Have To Lead This Race

My day begins without you near
I call your name, but can you hear?
The echo that repeats is clear
The message that I've come to fear

I try to bargain and to deal
But my mind won't let me heal
My heart will have to lead this race
My mind just can't keep up this pace

Routines repeated one by one
The same old this and that is done
And each one has lost all its fun
You're gone and with you the sun

Friends and family think of you
They loved you, this I knew
Others now have fun things new
But I remain the color blue

I try to bargain and to deal
But my mind won't let me heal

A Journey Through Mourning

My heart will have to lead this race
My mind just can't keep up this pace

The future seems so draped in black
It used to show colors stacked
I just don't seem to have the knack
To let you go and find my way back

It's not a matter for my mind
To think, to ponder, toe the line
It's more a matter of the heart
To hold and cradle, my sweetheart

I try to bargain and to deal
But my mind won't let me heal
My heart will have to lead this race
My mind just can't keep up this pace

It was my heart that let you go
So let that, also, let you know
You're tucked inside the only place
That mind and matter can't erase

The mind is good for many tasks
But healing hearts is one it lacks
My heart will have to lead this race
My mind could not keep up this pace

I'll carry you to places far
I'll reach and let you touch that star
I'll live this life with you inside
Till my heart finds the other side

No more bargain, no more deal
No more mind to help me heal
My heart will have to lead this race
You're tucked inside that special place

Even though Tom planned to leave Arizona, I think we both wanted to re-establish the good and decent relationship we enjoyed prior to Jack's illness. To do this, I searched for ways to keep Tom's presence in my life, even a limited presence, but I wasn't successful. His visits to my home became infrequent, and, if I had to guess why, it was because they were too painful for him. My home reminded him of his father.

Unfortunately, he and I couldn't mourn in private, apart from his wife and daughter. If the process had been able to stay between the two of us, we might have come to a more satisfactory and complete resolution of our strained relationship, to establish a new way of interacting. But grieving isn't simple. An incident, early November 2005, made me decide to go in another direction: I pulled back.

Tom, Karrin, and I were sitting at the kitchen counter in Tom's home. Karrin was two weeks away from having a baby. Madison was being disruptive, the way five year olds can be, and Karrin reprimanded her, after which I jokingly said, "And you want *another* one?"

Tom laughed and said, "I was kind of wondering the same thing myself." Karrin said to me, "If you ever say anything like that to me again, I'm going to really get mad." She was *not* laughing.

"I will probably continue to make these types of jokes in the future," I said.

Dear Jack,

I marvel at how well you were able to deal with these family situations. Please know I am trying. I know other times you would have a quick rebuttal to Karrin—you were so very good at that—one of the few people who could so adequately put the "Karrins" of this world in their proper place. I too may have a rebuttal one of these days, so wish me well.

Your John Boy

I thought, *This wouldn't be happening if Jack were here.* He would have been the miracle worker he always was. He could intercept and diffuse errant comments with either a sharp retort or a vacant silence that made attackers wonder why they wasted their rancor on someone so completely disinterested in anything they had to say.

But Jack wasn't there. And without him, sparks caused by disrespect aimed at me could easily turn into fire, and I would have no one to put out the flames. I didn't want to chance this, so I decided the solution was to emotionally distance myself from Tom's family.

> *Forgiveness—The act of forgiving (excuse for a fault or an offense; to renounce anger or resentment against); pardon.*

Later that evening, Tom and I had a long conversation about what had transpired. I told him I was aware Jack's death had changed the way our family interacted, and I acknowledged that I wouldn't dream of assuming Jack's role, because I didn't have his personality. I said, "I love you, Tom, and I understand that you need to focus on your family."

I did not want Tom to have to choose between maintaining his relationship with me and upsetting Karrin. (Grief had revealed still another grim facet of its personality.) I planned to leave him alone from here on out, and allow him to have what he needed, even though this meant pain for me.

This was the one and only time I talked to Tom about my pain and frustration over his plans to move. A year after this, I came to accept his decision, and, a short time later, forgiveness worked its magic on a want-to-be father and a pseudo son. (My relationship with Karrin is still strained, but I'm confident time will work on this. We have our differences, but that has never gotten in the way of me regarding her as a wonderful mother to Jack's grandchildren.)

To this day, I haven't received a response to a question I asked Tom: "If I had died and not your father, would you have left *him* and moved to Michigan?"

I See You In Myself

Your face I cannot feel or see but clothes you wore remain
The space you filled is all about but it's not quite the same
What we had then when you were here was special and unique
What I have now that you are gone has left me here to seek

I had to clean the memories out and place them on a shelf
My heart has been stored away like a plastic Christmas elf
I hope my heart will not grow old there, sitting in the dark
The memories that I placed it with were meant to heal a heart

My heart and soul remember well the items on that shelf
You touched and wore what I now store; I see you on the shelf

I could not bear to see them go, these items that you graced
I could not bear to let them stay; I had to find a place
The heart that had to watch you die, now had to do the rest
With loving hands and broken heart I pressed them to my chest

Pictures, wallets, rings and chains plus strands of golden locks
With teardrops falling on my cheeks I placed them in that box
I slipped in all the memories, each item that was you
And then I took this broken heart and left that with you too

My heart and soul remember well the items on that shelf
You touched and wore what I now store; I see you on the shelf

I know I put that box away, up there upon that nook
But somehow I still find you in strange places that I look
I saw you in the mirror staring back at me today
A piece of you had found its way to linger and to stay

The little things you said and did could not be hidden there
To boxes on a shelf so high my memories are so clear
The heart I had so gently placed in boxes there to rest
Had found its way down off that shelf and back into my chest

The you who moved, walked and talked was not up on the shelf
That box could not hold what you were; I see you in myself
I see you in the mirror staring back at me today
A piece of you had found its way to linger and to stay

The you that moved, walked and talked was not up on that shelf
That box could not hold what you were; I see you in myself

My heart and soul remember well the items on that shelf
You touched and wore what I now store; I see you in myself

In November, Karrin delivered her second daughter, Mia. How lovely! She has Jack's eyes, her face was Jack's face when he was a baby. I see her as another Jackie O. Jack knew she was going to be born. He'd predicted her birth in a clairvoyant moment, one morning in February 2005.

At the time we all blew it off as another one of Jack's delusions. I was sitting with him in his hospital room, talking about Madison, when he insisted he had two granddaughters.

"No, Jack," I said. "Madison is your one and only granddaughter."

"Madison *and* Sophia."

"You are wrong. You're having a delusion. Madison is your only grandchild."

"You're the one who's wrong. I have two, Madison and Sophia!"

"Fine. I'll prove it to you." I called Karrin, and she tried to talk some sense into Jack, but he refused to give in; nothing was going to change his mind.

And then, four months after Jack's death, Mia arrived! Jack had seen the future, seen past his physical demise. Her name was not Sophia, but she was a girl, and Jack had not been delusional. He had always possessed a sixth sense, and it was apparently unaffected by the brain tumor.

Little Jackie O arrived just in time; her birth nudging all of us to feel hopeful again. She glows for us the way Jack's personal ray of sunshine, Madison, always glowed for him.

> *"He who learns must suffer. And even in our sleep, pain that cannot forget falls drop by drop upon the heart, and in our own despair, against our will, comes wisdom to us by the awful grace of God."*
>
> Aeschylus

11.

Revelation: The Hummingbird's Sweet Smile

Skeptics dismissed my revelations as flukes, wishes, or lucky coincidences. I knew this because whenever I recounted the experiences that led to my revelations, I could read the disbelief in their eyes. But I am *sure* what happened was real. Death, loss, and grieving had opened my eyes and heart to the simplicity and beauty I had ignored before Jack died. Mourning had restored my childlike way of looking at the world.

When March of 2006 began to bloom, painting bougainvillea, Mexican Bird of Paradise, and night-blooming cereus on the desert, Jack had been physically gone from my presence for almost eight months.

Inspired by spring's freshness, I subjected my otherwise clean home to deeper scrubbing and, as I did this, found a tiny "something" lodged between the mopboard and wall in the living room. An unpopped popcorn seed. Most people would think, *So what, it's just a particle of food,* but I knew it represented much more than that. I reverently picked up this sacred seed and placed it in my dresser drawer, next to another popcorn seed I had found.

Revelation—Something revealed. A dramatic disclosure of something not previously known or realized. A manifestation of divine will or truth.

Popcorn seeds represent memories of my life with Jack. His favorite snack food. Saturday trips to the movies. A rented movie viewed at home, with my two favorite companions, Jack and Dusky, on either side of me, eating countless bowls of popcorn. There were always seeds—reminders of a day well spent—left in the bowl.

We continued our ritual after Jack became blind. He could use his right hand to feed himself, so I set the bowl at his left side, and he would reach into it, shovel up a handful of popcorn and dump it into his mouth.

As time passed, his left side became weaker, and so did his control, so sometimes the popcorn—and the bowl—found its way to the floor. When Jack could no longer feed himself, he still ate popcorn; I fed it to him. I couldn't expect him to go without it; it was too special to him, and, besides, I loved helping him this way.

What movie were we watching (by this time, Jack was "listening" to movies) when this seed made its way behind the mopboard? Could I remember the incident? Did it bounce and land there after Jack spilled popcorn, or had he spit it out? (Apparently blindness made him unaware of his surroundings, so he expelled seeds at will—to "seed" the carpet.) How it got there doesn't matter; what matters is that I found it, that it brought up reminders of who Jack was. In that kernel lay elements of his life as well as stories of unbelievable joy created throughout our life together. To others it was a speck, a crumb of food, but to me it was a large piece of Jack.

Before Jack's death, I would have never believed this much sorrow, pain, joy, and laughter could be bound to an unassuming little popcorn seed.

A few days later, another seed appeared, this time on our bedroom floor, in the exact spot where Jack's hospice bed had been, where My Banana Bread Man had been lying when he died. Finding it was not a coincidence, or the result of wishful thinking, because a few days earlier I had scoured every inch of this room. I would not have missed this popcorn seed. This was Jack's doing.

I placed this seed with the other two in my dresser. Now I have three popcorn seeds to remind me of Jack.

It's Just A Lonely Popcorn Seed

Each time I think I have moved on to forge a life brand new
Some speck of what we had appears and I remember you
It may be something simple and appear to no one else
Of any great importance but to me it holds such wealth

It's just a lonely popcorn seed leftover from a feast
But in that small hard kernel rests the you that's deceased

I know you're not all tucked away inside that yellow crumb
But in that tiny hardened shell lies memories, joy and fun
And even when the road was dark and illness came to stay
Those bowls of fresh popped kernels sat right there on your tray

Sometimes I think there's nothing left to remind me of the fun
When something small like popcorn shells let in memory's sun
Today I was reminded twice of you and what we shared
By simple specks of fallen food by seeds spit to mid-air

It's just a lonely popcorn seed leftover from a feast
But in that small hard kernel rests the you that's deceased

Popcorn was a special thing for both of us to share
At movies on a Saturday or home resting in chairs
Remember how you liked the butter and extra salt, for spice
It had to be a large bag and a soda full of ice

I know you're not all tucked away inside that yellow crumb
But in that tiny hardened shell lies memories, joy and fun
Today I was reminded twice of you and what we shared

By simple specks of fallen food by seeds spit to mid-air

It's just a lonely popcorn seed leftover from a feast
But in that small hard kernel rests the you that's deceased

Each time I think I have moved on to forge a life brand new
Some speck of what we had appears and I remember you
It may be something simple and appear to no one else
Of any great importance but to me it holds such wealth

It's just a lonely popcorn seed leftover from a feast
But in that small hard kernel rests the you that's deceased

One sunny afternoon, a week after the last popcorn incident, I was leaving my parents' Scottsdale home, when several hummingbirds in teeny jet streams whisked past me. One broke from the group and landed, not quite two feet in front of me, on an exposed lower branch of a bush. Then this small, yet powerful, bird demanded my attention. "Hey there!" it said. "Look this way! Can you see me?"

Of course I could see him. I was transfixed.

Then he seemed to say, "Come closer, John Boy."

I called to my parents, "Look at that hummingbird! Have you ever known one to stop and simply sit there and look at you? Hummingbirds don't linger."

They, too, had never seen a sight such as this.

I was incredibly animated, talking loudly, my hands waving, but the hummingbird did not scare. Instead, it gazed wistfully at me, beckoning me to move a little closer. I obliged him.

How can your little image hold me frozen here in place?
Who are you little bird so rare, who should vanish without a trace?
Why do you sit so still, so close and look at me and wait?
Why do you show me colors bright, why do you hesitate?

Either I'd become more in tune with nature and all it entails, or Jack had found yet another way to gently hold me in his arms. Perhaps my increased sensitivity led me to see Jack, or, perhaps, Jack led me to be more sensitive. Maybe both.

I moved closer, and a color show commenced. My visitor fluttered his wings, displaying resplendent shades of fuchsia, blue, and green. (I was amazed he did this while perched on a branch, which is not what hummingbirds are programmed to do.) I reached out to him, but instead of flying away, he kept performing at least a minute longer.

And then my magnified glance at nature's face ended. I walked past him, and he took flight, jetting into the sky. Smiling, I turned to my parents and said, "Must be Jack."

My mother agreed, and chills ran up and down her arms.

*How can your little image hold me frozen here in
  place?*
*Who are you little bird so rare, who should vanish
  without a trace?*
*Why do you sit so still, so close and look at me and
  wait?*
*Why do you show me colors bright, why do you
  hesitate?*

I had seen photographs depicting what I witnessed, but I'd never been privy to a private, front row performance of a Jack Color Show! I had witnessed a miracle, as small as a bird, but a miracle just the same. I believe he flew to me to provide encouragement, in the only means possible. Jack had held me in his arms.

Nature had a knack for helping me go on, and for sending messages to me. Nature was reassuring me that I was going to find Jack.

The Hummingbird's Sweet Smile

*I strolled on down this little path and suddenly you
  were there*
*Your little friends you flew here with had gone to
  who knows where*
You returned and landed on a branch for me to see
And little did I realize that you would smile on me

*Just like the life we shared for years with color and
  with style*
*Remembered in the visit from the hummingbird's
  sweet smile*

At first, you were so quiet as I stopped to notice you
And then your little head would twist and turn to show me blue
Startled and unsure of what to make of you still here
I took just one step closer and you beckoned "Closer, Dear"

The show would now begin as you fluttered tiny wings
The sun now glistened on you, clearly asking you to sing
The color show of pinks and blues and greens burst in midair
The tiny bird from who knows where was showing something rare

Just like the life we shared for years with color and with style
Remembered in the visit from the hummingbird's sweet smile

I took just one step closer and you beckoned "John Boy, see"
And then your little head would twist and turn to say, "It's me"
The show continued onward as you fluttered tiny wings
The sun now glistened on you clearly asking you to sing

The color show of pinks and blues and greens burst in midair
The tiny bird from who knows where was showing something rare
Suddenly you vanished as I walked into your space
You were gone from sight again and had vanished without trace

Just like the life we shared for years with color and with style
Remembered in the visit from the hummingbird's sweet smile

How did your little image hold me frozen here in place?
Who were you little bird so rare, who should vanish without a trace?
Why did you sit so still, so close and look at me and wait?
Why did you show me colors bright, why did you hesitate?

Just like the life we shared for years with color and with style
Remembered in the visit from the hummingbird's sweet smile

Throughout spring and early summer, I continued to happen upon revelations. And I was glad for them, because they helped me get through still more firsts without Jack: Easter, his birthday, and a trip to Norway, Michigan.

That May I traveled to Norway to present a

$2000.00 "Jack's Memorial Scholarship" during Norway High School's commencement program. The money came from well wishers who'd donated to it in lieu of sending flowers to Jack's Celebration of Life ceremony. I felt this scholarship provided a lasting connection to Jack as well as a way to pay tribute to the community that helped raise him. It also stood as a testament to his past, a symbol of his spirit, a way to carry his legacy into the future.

Applicants, who planned to attend beautician school, submitted essays based on the topic "What tolerance towards others means to me." The young woman who won wrote a wonderful, high-caliber essay that I'd easily attribute to a college student. Through her writing she unknowingly described the essence of Jack.

I chose to honor Jack at this high school commencement because, in deference to his mother, I didn't want to have any other sort of official memorial celebration. Jack's mother (85 years) was still living in Norway. She was suffering from Alzheimer's disease, so she was unaware her precious son had died. I didn't want her to learn the truth because I knew it would hasten her death. (This pretense is another cruelty associated with Jack's illness and death.) To this day, his mother still believes he's alive. If his name is mentioned, she says, "Jack? Oh, he called me yesterday."

When I presented the scholarship, I gave a speech in which I shared the message of Jack's life: live in love, live in the moment, and perform tiny deeds of good action.

It pleased me that Jack's life was celebrated in the most public of arenas, and that I could memorialize him as the good and decent man he was, one of the shiniest examples of Norway, Michigan's, native sons. My Banana Bread Man was gone, but I found a piece of him when I went back to his hometown.

I decided to also share Jack's legacy with the community he loved, Scottsdale, Arizona, so I established the Jack Orler Heal-A-Heart Program, an open-ended funding program. Through this, I make a $250 contribution (gift) every quarter to a community service organization dedicated to improving the quality of life for others. I also make direct contributions to individuals in need.

This program has provided food/meals to underprivileged people, assisted families of cancer patients, and has helped the fight for diversity and tolerance. It has also provided support for the Hospice of the Valley. There are limitless possibilities for where the funds can go; I ask only that they go to people and organizations whose lives, or activities, reflect Jack's loving and caring spirit.

Everyone who receives funds from this program receives a letter from me and the following:

Jack Orler Heal-A-Heart Program
One Moment At A Time

Jack was a man of great compassion and love

Always looking for the best in everyone who entered his life

Caring about people, family and friends, was how he lived his life

Kindness was delivered in every action and fiber of his being

Over the years he helped man; although he's gone now, his legacy continues

Rarely did he fail to show us all a smiling face, now a helping hand is offered

Largely due to his earning potential this program is possible

Eagerly, this program seeks to help heal A Heart-A Soul-A Mind

Remembering Jack and what he stood for is this program's only request

Hearts, Souls and Minds are meant to be healed with each gift given

Each gift is given with a loving heart, in memory of Jack

Accept the gift given and live your life as if today were your last day to live

Learn to live each moment of your life In The Precious Present

Avail yourself to your fellow man; someday return this favor received

Helping those in need—or less fortunate—is the goal of this program

Every time you help someone else, you help yourself, inside

Around every corner is someone in need

Right here and now is how to live your life—not yesterday and tomorrow

To help you get to where you're going is why this gift is given

Perhaps positive feelings and hope can come out of Jack's untimely death

Regardless of race, creed, or sexual orientation, you are eligible to be gifted

Organizations might get these monies, but the preference will be for people

Gifts given through the program are meant to Heal A Heart-A Soul-A Mind

Right up until the moment of Jack's death he had a smile on his face

Are you prepared to start living your Life One Moment At A Time?

Make sure to remember Jack; he made this gift possible

In a variety of ways, Jack remains alive to me. I only have to see a popcorn seed or a hummingbird to be reminded that what he used to be still exists. All I have to do to see his face again is share his loving spirit with others.

As soon as possible, I will have two trees planted in Jack's and my honor in Fountain Hills. They'll stand in remembrance of Jack, and will commemorate the special love and relationship we fostered. At their base, I will place a plaque that bears our names and the words "We will meet again."

"Hope is the thing with feathers
That perches in the soul
And sings the tune without words
And never stops at all."
          Emily Dickinson

12.

Remembrance: Always Mine... Times Two

How much more would you like me to endure before you remove this black cloud of death from my doorstep? I asked the god inside me. I didn't receive an answer. It was July 3, 2006, and I had just returned from a day in Phoenix. Earlier, as the sun baked the desert earth, the man Jack called "My Timmy" died. The man my friends and family knew as an Angel of Mercy had been swimming in the pool at his apartment complex when he had an epileptic seizure and drowned.

Timmy hadn't had a seizure in years, so I didn't understand why he had to have one while in the pool. I still don't understand it. I realize accidents happen, and that often those we love are taken from us for no reason, that dear friends can be here one day and gone the next.

I realize these things, but I can't comprehend why the good die young. Why should their lives be cut short? Why do the best vanish from our sight, while the cruel and unkind remain among us? Why do those people still breathe and take up space that the good people stolen from us should be allowed to occupy? I don't have any answers.

So one month before the one-year anniversary of

Jack's death, I arranged and conducted a tribute for another dear man, which was attended by many of Jack's and my friends. As it worked out, in the hard months leading up to Jack's death, many of Jack's friends became my friends (some of these friendships have continued), and, in the process, they got to know Timmy. They appreciated the numerous hours he spent with Jack, understanding this gave me relief from care giving and, thereby, helped me regain some of my sanity.

During Timmy's tribute I said, "Timmy fed Jack, he helped him to the bathroom, and he helped me care for him. He was a good friend to me and to Jack."

It didn't seem fair to me that this Angel of Mercy was going to have the opportunity to find My Banana Bread Man before I did. But I vowed to keep searching for him, anyway. I knew it was going to take a lifetime.

In May, a few days before I presented Jack's scholarship in Michigan, I had to say good-bye to Tom and his family. They started off for Michigan while I was in Norway, and they arrived there six hours after I completed my memorial address and scholarship presentation. Their new life was starting in Michigan, while mine, without Tom, Madison, or Mia was starting in Arizona.

This was more than 2 years ago (as of this writing), and Tom's physical absence from my life is still painful. I miss seeing the essence of Jack in his eyes, his nose, legs, arms, and especially his hands, which are identical to Jack's: large and masculine. When Tom opens a sealed jar, I see Jack, his powerful hands wrenching the lid off, his face contorting as he twists. And Tom's smile. Reminiscent of his father's. And his personality? It's obvious he's My Banana Bread Man's son.

I said good-bye to Tom, trusting that, although he did not see me as a father figure, he would at least see me as a good friend deserving of connection to his family, trusting that he would eventually realize that what he viewed as my harsh insistence that he visit Jack more frequently and spend higher quality time with him, came from love.

I hoped he would realize that love requires people to undertake uncomfortable and difficult tasks, and that he would come to understand how much I loved Jack and how devastating it was to lose him. I also hoped one day he would come to terms with how devastating his father's death was for him.

When I said good-bye, I also trusted time would allow him to remember the spirit and essence of what Jack represented, and that he would find ways to pass this essence on to Madison and Mia, because I believe death cannot steal what heritage grows, just as "death cannot steal what the heart knows."

A few days after Jack's death, Madison, Tom, and Karrin dined at a Chinese restaurant, and at the end of the meal Madison picked up her fortune cookie and said, "Mommy, Daddy, the fortune in here is from Papa Jack." (Children are much more in tune with the death process than we give them credit for.) Her innocent reflection on Jack's spirit inspired me to give her and Mia a special Christmas present that year: six sterling silver Lenox fortune cookies, each containing a message from Papa Jack.

Dear Madison and Mia,

This year you have received six Lenox fortune cookies from me, your Papa Jack. These are personal messages sent, with love, from me to you.

The plan is for you to get these fortunes from me each year; all you have to do is return the cookies to John by Halloween. He will ensure that new messages from me are created, tucked inside, and sent back to you by Christmas. This will be a Christmas tradition called "Fortunes From The Heart."

You are now part of this Christmas tradition, so that I can be with you always, through the written messages you receive in your Fortunes From The Heart.

Here are a few fortunes from me, right now. You can always count on these permanent fortunes from me to you:

"I will ... watch over you every day"
"I will ... always be with you"
"I will ... see you someday"
"I will ... love you forever"
"I will ... always be part of your life"

Each year, as you open these cookies, remember me, and

"I will ... live forever in your heart, your mind, your memory."

Love You Always,

                         Your Papa Jack

Upon my death, Madison will receive another gift: the quilt my sister Barbara (Green Bay, WI) stitched together for me, using fabric from a few of Jack's favorite shirts. I imagine it will keep me warm for many years, and when I die, it will keep Madison warm, provide her with a piece of her heritage, and provide a soft reminder of being held in her grandfather's arms. When I think about this, the pendulum of my emotions swings beautifully between deep love and contentment.

> *Remembrance—The act of remembering. The state of being remembered. Something serving to celebrate or honor the memory of a person or event. The length of time over which one's memory extends.*

While mourning Jack, I was repeatedly comforted by remembering him, spreading his essence in celebration of his life, and by extending "tiny deeds of good action," a concept I adapted from Soygal Rinpoche's *The Tibetan Book of Living and Dying*. Rinpoche says: "Do not overlook tiny good actions, thinking they are of no benefit; even tiny drops of water in the end will fill a huge vessel." I added "deeds" to "tiny good actions" to reflect the lovely small things Jack did for people—not because he expected to be rewarded, but because he was Jack.

Tiny deeds of good action were ever present in his life. He could always be counted on to escort an elderly customer from her car into his salon, work wonders with her silver hair, then escort her back to her car. If a customer was ailing and unable to travel to his salon, he went to her, it didn't matter where; either her home or care facility was fine. He never failed to give her hair a fresh appearance and her attitude a new face.

Jack was always a good one for baking and delivering his culinary wonders—his famous banana bread, for example—to friends, family, and customers, on any/all holidays: Christmas, Thanksgiving, New Year's Eve, birthdays, you name it. He was a giver and a doer who gave and did more with his short time on earth than many who live decades longer; moreover, he bestowed his deeds, actions of devotion, on me and our home.

My partner was as good a mate to me as he was a grandfather, father, son, and friend to others. I state as much in a line in one of my poems: "What he always was to you, was also always mine ... times two." There is no better way to remember Jack than to spread his tiny deeds of good actions, simple deeds that cost me nothing but have far-reaching effects.

I made a list of tiny deeds of good action and began to implement them:

Offer a compliment in place of a criticism, especially when what I say could fall on the ears of someone who is in pain.

Bake, using one of Jack's favorite recipes, then give the results to someone hungry for a treat or conversation.

Visit an ill, dying, or lonely person in a nursing home or other care facility.

Guide an elderly person across a street. Carry his/her groceries.

Transport an elderly person to and from medical appointments.

Smile and say hello to someone who seems to need a pick-me-up.

Donate my excess goods—clothing, furniture, items Timmy left to me but I don't have a use for—to those less fortunate than I.

Volunteer my time and energy to a cause dear to my heart.

Hold the door open for someone.

I was also comforted when I chose to remember and memorialize Jack through carefully selected and distributed gifts. For example, on the Halloween immediately following Jack's death, I gathered a group of his dear friends at my home to create potpourri out of the roses from his Celebration of Life ceremony. We soaked them in Drakkar Noir cologne, and then everyone took some potpourri so they could scent their home with Jack's essence.

Those who had assisted during Jack's illness received a special Christmas gift in 2005: a beautifully bound book of photographs taken at various Arizona locations. Jack's photo was on the cover, and there was an inscription inside that read: "Picture of Jack on 9-19-04, living, as he always did, in the moment. So now he would like you to remember him by living in the moment. He loved you." I also had specially designed bookmarks made; they, too, mention Jack's ability to live in the moment. I mailed them with my Christmas letters.

Tiny deeds of good action can take the form of words. For example, I spelled out my appreciation to the loving people who were my core support during Jack's illness and after his death.

> Dear Mom and Dad, Sharon, Judi, Steve and Paul, Cathy, Mick, Brenda and Jack,
>
> The fact that you are receiving this letter means that you hold a special place in my heart.
>
> Following the death of anyone—in my case,

Jack—a person travels a lonely road, but the road is traveled with some individuals who have a connection to the person who is grieving, and they have hearts bigger than themselves. For each person who suffers the loss of a loved one—for me, my soul mate and partner—there are some friends and family who cannot bear the pain and suffering you feel, and they opt to distance themselves from you. Each of you has graciously decided to walk this path with me. It is time for me to thank each and every one of you.

Mom and Dad—Scottsdale, Arizona—The strength of my soul, the teachers of my "self," the wisdom of years lived. You are the essence of how to live, and you've done so well. You are what parents should always be to a child. I love you.

Sharon—Scottsdale, Arizona—I've known you only two years at the most, a neighbor two doors down from me, my confidant. To say you understand me would be an understatement; to say you care would be a fact. A good person. A mother with two beautiful children, and who has a neighbor who thinks the world of her. Where did you come from, my special friend?

Judi—Vulcan, Michigan—Strong and true, mother of two grown women, widow, in constant contact and always urging me forward. Suffered the same unbearable loss of a mate. You know my pain. You have been there, and you care. Initially a friend of Jack's, now one of my best. How sweet you are, my dear Judi.

Steve and Paul—Scottsdale, Arizona—

A Journey Through Mourning

Long-time partners, like Jack and I. Your relationship may not have suffered this pain, but in your relationship you can understand the devastation this type of loss would entail. You can sense it, and I feel you understand where I am. Accomplished artists. Talented. Hearts of Gold. You are dear friends.

Cathy—Ashland, Oregon—Sister, actress, a truer friend I could never find. You call me and counsel me through my deepest emotions. You have the wisdom of a parent and the wings of an Angel. Younger than I, you know me inside and out. Loved My Jack as a brother, felt, and still feels, the sting of his loss. You understand exactly where I am, and believe in me. Love you, Kiddo.

Mick—Scottsdale, Arizona—Artist, musician, talented. You've experienced the loss of a partner, know the depths of its pain. Wise beyond your years. New to my life, but connected somehow. You urge me forward, tell me that "Life is for the Living" and say that message is from Jack. You speak Jack's name easily. You're self confident, strong. I'm not sure why you have entered my life, but I'm glad you're here.

Brenda—Fountain Hills, Arizona—Manicurist. Long-time deep and trusted friend of Jack's. Attached so deeply to Jack that his spirit glows around you. You are a special connection to him—and to me. You cry with me, remember with me, will never forget him. If I was his soul mate, you were his soul sister. I am connected to you always, My Dear Brenda.

Jack—Wherever Heaven is, or What Heaven is, you're on this journey with me, my soul mate, lover, partner, the best that life had to give. See the list above, baby, see who is taking this voyage thru grief with me, so closely, who is pulling me, prodding me, encouraging me, and loving me. Save for them—for me—a special place in your heart. A special place in "Your Heaven."

To all of you, I want to extend my deepest appreciation for who you are and what you mean to me. You have allowed "steam to be released from this boiling pot." You are the spirit of what friendship and love is all about. You are all Good Men and Women. Friends can help keep grief flowing, and you have been those friends to me.

It says in The Apocrypha that "A faithful friend is the medicine of life." You've been that to me.

My love and thanks to each of you,

John

As I've said, I have performed tiny deeds of good action in remembrance of Jack, and I will continue to do this, yet I want his essence to extend beyond my lifetime. To do this, I established a trust, which, upon my death, will provide financial assistance to people who have been important to us. It is meant to help our family members through their remaining years, but, more importantly, it is to serve as a legacy of the fine human being I had the good fortune of calling my partner. The trust will also continue to assist organizations I will have contributed to before my death. I expect these funds will last forever—or as long as society as I know it exists.

I have two stipulations for those gifted. The first, honor Jack by living in a meaningful manner. The second, remember the individual in whose name they receive this money—Jack.

> *"The only truly dead are those who have been forgotten."*
> Jewish Saying

13.

Hope: Finding My Banana Bread Man, Finding Myself

A year of firsts ended, and I was alive. I had miraculously survived a whole year without Jack physically by my side. I'd made it through one year of grieving, and I don't know how I did it.

> My Dear Jack,
> The date I thought I would never reach is less than 48 hours away, the date of your death one year ago. That sounds so foreign to me. How can there be a date that has your death attached to it? How can you really be gone? Each day when I wake up I am reminded once again that your beautiful presence is no longer around me, yet, as I said in one of the poems I wrote about you: "I see you in myself." I really do see you in myself, and I guess this is how you are continuing to live through me.
> I love you, always and forever, my Sweet Jackie O.

It became clear to me that Jack had never stopped being my "soft place to land," that he had helped me survive 12 months of hell on earth. I wondered if getting through the year was possible because our love survived death.

It then occurred to me that death was transforming me, and this was opening up a means for Jack to reach deep into my dreams to visit and touch me. This heavenly contact was a sign I was starting to recover and was moving closer to finding My Banana Bread Man. I felt the pendulum gently swinging, giving me moments of peace.

Slumber's Gentle Ride

I wake with dreams of you each day; I feel you touch my side
Your fingers seek my body still in slumber's gentle ride
You whisper, "Please don't cry for me," but tears start to fall
The real truth now startles me, my eyes, through tears, recall

My pillow moist with sorrow's juice I feel you touch my face
Your fingers seek my body still in slumber's gentle space
Each time I try to start the day your voice it calls me back
I tell you "Keep me by your side" let morning light go black

I wake with dreams of you each day; I feel you touch my side
Your fingers seek my body still in slumber's gentle ride

Your fingers seek my body still in slumber's gentle ride

I finally rise to start the day; I feel you touch my side
A day just like the last one, Dear; it's like the rising tide
I pour my morning coffee knowing that you took yours black
Straight from the pot was what you liked, the condiments it lacked

Your mouth, it touched the cup I use; I feel you touch my lips
I use the mug you always loved, remembering with each sip
The paths we shared together, walking one step at a time
Recalling precious moments with your hand entwined with mine

I wake with dreams of you each day; I feel you touch my side
Your fingers seek my body still in slumber's gentle ride
Your fingers seek my body still in slumber's gentle ride

The pieces of each day slip by; I feel you touch my heart
Your presence here is constant now; I knew you'd find my heart
The life we shared is gone, I know, a new one did begin

*I found a way to keep you close, and now my heart
  can sing*

*The pieces of each day slip by; I feel you touch my
  heart*
*Your presence here is constant now; I knew you'd
  find my heart*
*I find you in the places that we share our whole life
  through*
*I keep you in my memory, where I treasure me and
  you*

*I wake with dreams of you each day; I feel you
  touch my side*
*Your fingers seek my body still in slumber's gentle
  ride*
*Your fingers seek my body still in slumber's gentle
  ride*

The books and articles I read on grieving assured me that on the first anniversary of Jack's death the worst part of the grieving process would be over. But on August 1, 2006, the first day of my *second* year without Jack, I was in as much pain as I was a year earlier! I couldn't help scolding myself for counting on feeling better: *The first year is over, and now the only thing I have to look forward to is a year of "seconds." Do I really expect to be able to go on as I had when Jack was at my side?*

I was in danger of losing hope ... again. And hope is a terrible thing to lose. I knew this as I'd already lost and found it several times over the previous months, beginning with Jack's diagnosis in October 2004. And hope was not only lost, it was also dashed, forgotten, and abandoned. Terminal cancer has a way of eating away the flesh of its victims *and* the heart and soul of their loved ones.

So much is hoped, wished, and prayed for, that when death claims the one you love, you don't have any hope left; it takes super human efforts from your heart and soul, and months of grieving, to restore it. I am thankful my core of support and other dear friends helped me get it back.

Hope—To wish for something with expectation of its fulfillment. To have confidence; trust. To look forward to with confidence or expectation. To expect and desire. One that is a source of or reason for hope.

Despite how desperate Jack's situation became, he never lost hope. He kept trying, for example, even after the tumor began to rob him of his cognitive skills, and he sometimes forgot how old he was. To help him, I drilled him on his age, but this wasn't enough to help him remember, so we came up with a cue: When he had trouble remembering his age, I said, "double nickels," and he would say "55." After enough repetition, Jack's age was again cemented in his memory.

Another example of the strength of his hope is a beautiful exchange that took place between Jack, my parents, and me during his March 2005 hospitalization. I asked Jack, "How old are you?" He hesitated, so I gave him his cue.

"Oh yes," he said. "I'm 55."

Then my father immediately asked, "Jack, how old are you?"

"Am I on concrete or grass?"

This perplexed me, so I said, "I don't understand the question, but ... you're on neither." Then I jokingly added, "Well, what if you were on the water?"

"How far am I from the shore?"

"About a mile."

"In what direction am I going?"

"South."

Smirking, he gave us his answer. "Then I'm getting younger!"

I can still see his boyish grin of satisfaction, an emblem of his ever-present sense of humor as well as a perfect example of the beacon of hope that continued to burn brightly within him, even as my beacon was beginning to dim.

I told myself that, as sick as Jack was, he never gave up, so, even though I was in considerable mental pain, I, too, could never give up. I didn't want to stop seeing the colors of his humor and feeling the hope which permeated his life. I might not have been getting younger—like Jack was when he sailed south on the water—but I had hope, and for this I could thank the love of my life.

Jack provided hope, comfort, and understanding while I struggled with several issues:

Denial. *Jack can't be dead. He can't be.* Every morning I woke up thinking he was still with me, and I had to remind myself he was gone ... forever.

Self-forgiveness, a difficult and continually unfolding process. This was the hardest thing to work through.

Anger at the unfairness of Jack's death. *This shouldn't have happened. I didn't deserve to have this happen to me.*

Resentment toward people whose lives continued

to be normal, while mine, mired in grief, was anything but normal.

Despair. *I am alone. How can I stumble through this maze of pain without Jack at my side?*

The fear there would be more reasons for sorrow. My parents were already in their mid-80s when Jack died, so their deaths weren't going to be that far in the future. I had always expected Jack would be with me when that time came. I also expected he'd keep Tom and me close to each other.

A few weeks after the first anniversary of Jack's death, I sent a short and pointed birthday message to Tom: "I never realized how your father's death had defined my place in your life." I was hurt because he had ignored my birthday, which fell one week before his. I read his neglect as a sign that I should close the door on our relationship and release him from any further expectations.

I felt Tom had already decided to close the door, so, in a last-ditch effort to make peace and get out from under the problems between us, I was going to let go of Tom and his daughters.

Tom's response was opposite of what I'd expected. He e-mailed me, asking questions and, most importantly, expressing his love. As it turned out, he hadn't called because he wanted to find out if *I* still loved *him*. This was the opening to a renewed relationship I'd been waiting for!

> Dear Tom,
> I wish you were closer so that we could talk in person. I wish you had not moved. I wish your father were still alive. I wish grandchildren were closer. I wish the last two years had never

happened. I wish I had my life back. I wish people could understand what it is like to lose half of yourself and be expected to continue—in short order—as if nothing had happened. I wish people would understand that grieving is a lifetime endeavor. I wish people would speak his name and remember him always and not try to hide him from me in their conversation. I wish your father were here—for you and for me.

Grieving is never an easy task, but I would certainly like to be able to grieve with you and share some of my deepest pain and my greatest joys. Yes, I believe there are unspoken issues between us, but perhaps with a little effort on both our parts we can resolve some of them—just you and I.

I look forward to a new beginning with you. Although it is difficult, I will certainly try to call you more; I know you will call me, after all, you are your father's son, with a phone growing out of your ear. Just as you were grateful for the birthday card because it was an indication to you that I care and want you as part of my life, I am grateful for your e-mail, as it reflects the same to me.

Love, John

The floodgates had opened! And throughout the following week, we talked and wrote to one another. We discussed our hurt feelings and festering wounds. I told Tom I was disappointed I didn't receive a Father's Day card from him, especially since his and Karrin's stepfathers had received such cards,

A Journey Through Mourning

and that in all the years I'd known him, I had been more like a father to him than any man other than Jack.

I told him Jack was my once-in-a-lifetime love, that he was irreplaceable and would always own a place in my heart that no one else will ever occupy. I said there's a chance I'll go on to find another person to love, with whom I'll share my life.

Tom and I might not have always seen things in the same light, but now we could talk about our differences. We'd both traveled a long way since Jack's death, taken different roads to arrive at this moment, but that didn't matter, because we had new hope for our relationship. (I know I will never be a father to him—not even a pseudo father—but I will always be able to call him a good friend with a huge heart; family dynamics will not allow us to form a deeper relationship.)

Eighteen months after Jack's death, I stepped away from mourning to look back and reflect on my progress. I had written copiously, and poems and letters had begun to pile up. When I re-read my poems, I saw they told the story of how I grieved for Jack. My Letters to Jack revealed I'd made progress and had begun to hope for a happy future. (The power of the pen as an integral counseling tool should never be overlooked.) I was emerging from darkness, what I thought would suck me into an early grave.

I realized I was learning to live again, forming a new relationship with Jack. I was even learning that I was able to smile without him physically at my side, however, I was *not* learning to forget what it felt like to be loved by him. My closest friends and family members also noticed my progression and hope. I was grateful for their feedback; after all, they had witnessed every step of my journey thus far. But it was still frustrating when people off-handedly spouted directives at me: "Let go of Jack. Bury the past. Forget. Spend more time reading the Bible." I couldn't understand why they persisted.

I was all too aware that the loss of a mate should never be washed away, or buried, as a means for recovery. A grieving soul learns to incorporate this loss and move forward, but the loss is never forgotten; it stays with you until your dying day. You just have to learn to live again. You craft a new relationship with the person who is gone. You learn to love and smile again. You strive to enjoy all that life has to offer, but you *never* forget.

Forgetting is like running away from a problem that's determined to hound you until you turn around and face it, acknowledge it, and feel the emotions associated with it. When you remember the past, and allow the pain to run its course, you survive to become healthy. When you remember, feel, and talk about your loss, you become reunited with the hope you thought you'd never see again, and you uncover the essence of your loved one whose physical presence is no longer obtainable.

On a Monday, a few days before Thanksgiving 2006, I visited with Brenda, one of Jack's co-workers who became my dear friend during the course of his illness. She dearly loved Jack. She loves *me* now, and she is one of those rare individuals who understands the magnitude of what it has meant to lose Jack.

For 19 years, Brenda rented space for her nail business in Jack's salon, his payment being a percentage of her earnings. She had always been a "free spirit," something I'm sure Jack loved about her. She led a laid-back life, and she lived in the spur of the moment—as opposed to being a planner, or devoted to building up riches. Jack didn't care how much she earned; he was completely delighted just to have her extraordinary presence in his salon.

I suppose a shrewd and money-hungry owner would not have given Brenda much of a chance—after all, they start a business to make money—but Jack never followed the rules of business. He followed his heart, and he devoted space to an individual not set to make a slew of money. Brenda, not her income, was important to him.

Around the time he was dismantling his salon, April 2004, Jack told me two people had each stiffed him out of $100.00. He could have easily confronted them to demand payment, however, he did nothing; he simply dismissed their actions as irresponsible, then forgave their debt. Money was not his god; it was kindness, love, and forgiveness. This meant he showed kindness and friendship to those who didn't deserve it. He followed his heart, and made a fine living doing so. Everything he touched turned to gold.

Brenda told me Jack had said to her, "I will always be your soft place to land," and she never forgot it. These nine simple words describe Jack's essence. He had been Brenda's soft place to land, and he was the same for several other people. What he was to others, he was to me ... times two.

While Brenda and I talked, it struck me that I was going to be okay, that I would go on breathing without Jack's physical presence in my life. It was then I realized our roles had reversed: instead of Jack offering me a soft place to land, I was prepared to offer *him* a soft place to land.

On that Monday afternoon, I opened my heart to Jack, and there he landed softly. This is where he will remain forever.

I see him in the mirror staring back at me today
A piece of him had found its way to linger and to stay

I still recall the hair of gold
How it parted, how it glowed
I still see those eyes of brown
How they turned my heart around

I still miss him by my side
He was my life's gentle ride
What he always meant to you
Was also always mine ... times two

I still see the distant land
Where I first saw that sweet man

I still see his eyes so brown
How they turned my heart around

I'm now his soft place to land
That sweet and gentle loving man

As I conclude *Finding My Banana Bread Man*, my journey through mourning is closer to complete. I have discovered that Jack was never truly lost. Death and grief had used the fact that I could not see him to fool me into believing he was gone forever. I now know love survives death, that it nourishes and shelters dormant hope until it is able to blossom again, that it lets you find what you're looking for. Love let me find Jack. It also let me find myself.

Time will never erase the pain of losing Jack. Even now, years after his death, when I hear one of our favorite songs, happen upon a roll of Winto Greens, or see Jack's smile in his granddaughters' eyes, I cry for him. And I will cry, repeatedly, until the end of my life.

I will always feel the sting of my broken heart, and I will continue to mourn for the part of me that vanished when Jack left. I will always miss him. Time won't erase the pain, but it will smooth its sharp edges.

For 27 years, Jack taught me how to live in the moment, and then he taught me how to die with grace. I am blessed to have known him, and I will love him forever because, from beginning to end, he was steadfast. He was My Jack, Sweet Jackie O, My Banana Bread Man.

> *"His noble face is more alive to me now than any of the faces of the living, and in his eyes I always see that light of transcendent wisdom and transcendent compassion that no power in heaven or earth can put out."*
> Sogyal Rinpoche

Epilogue

A night-blooming cereus cactus thrived in the yard outside the home Jack and I shared. Nurtured by Jack's love, it generally produced fragrant white flowers 2 or 3 times a year. (He nurtured everything and everyone in his life.) When Jack became ill, our cactus ceased blooming, fell dormant. It had joined me in mourning Jack.

Life is like the frost we see
It sometimes kills the beauty
And underneath the killing frost
Are memories of all that's lost

When frost has taken life from you
Erased and snatched what you grew
Remember how the sun would shine
How the rain would feed the vines

Death becomes what can be seen
But you still have memories of green

Today, 2 1/2 years after Jack's death, our cactus is flowering again, its blossoms full and aromatic. I believe this is a sign that I must live again. And I will. I will live and bloom in memory of Jack.

Jack's Banana Bread Recipe

Preheat oven to 350° F

Combine:
4 bananas, mashed
½ cup shortening
1 cup sugar
2 eggs
1 teaspoon salt
3 tablespoons milk
1 teaspoon soda—in milk
2 teaspoons baking powder
2 cups flour
½ cup walnuts

Pour into two regular size loaf pans
Sometimes Jack sprinkled cinnamon and sugar on top

Bake for 45 minutes

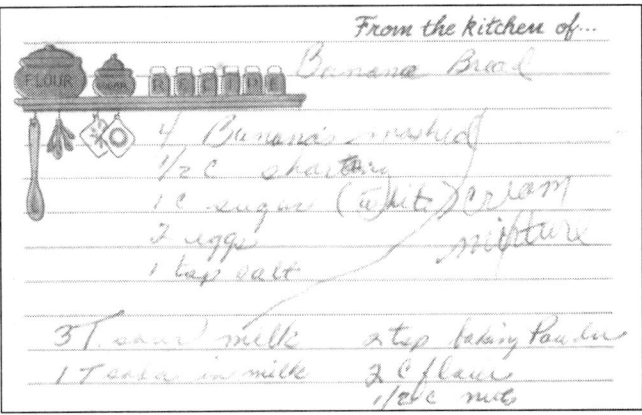

Jack's Banana Bread recipe. I miss everything about him, even his scribbled handwriting.

Memories of Green: Photographs

Jack—September 2004

Because he has been here I will be different than I would have been, and I will have to become his legacy. He travels with me into tomorrow.

Jack may have died, but love never ends.

*Even at three, he had an ever-present smile.
Jack, 3 years old, Norway, Michigan, 1952.*

I still recall the hair of gold—how it parted, how it glowed. Jack, 31 years old, 1980.

Jack being Jack, goofing off for the camera. We shared so many of these "I Love Lucy" moments.

Dusky, 1990. Note: By the time this photo was taken, he was already "King of the Walk."

Jack and Tom, early 1990s.
"I saw you shape and mold a son the two of us would raise. I saw a father's love grow strong and shape this young man's ways."

Dusky, Buck, and me, early 1991. Our household had a pecking order: Jack, followed by Dusky, Buck, and then me.

Me, Dusky, and Jack, Christmas 1989. Jack gave me Dusky as a birthday present, but within three months, he claimed Dusky was "his."

"And so I shared my gift of him ... with each and every one he trimmed." Jack at work, early 1990s.

Me, Tom, Dusky, and Jack, Christmas 1992.

Jack's dream house, the house we built in 1999, where he lived only five short years, where he died.

Jack's rule: He gets the first bite, Madison the second, and Dusky the third. Jack, Madison, and Dusky (I'm in the background), on Madison's first birthday, May 2001.

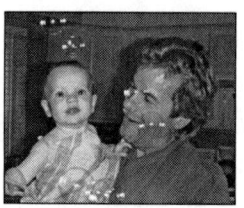

Madison's eyes are still identical to her Papa Jack's. Jack and Madison, 1 year old, 2001.

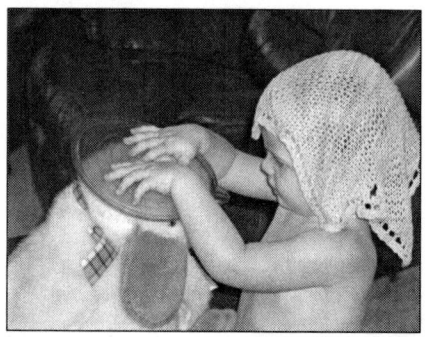

Madison, 2 years old, with a dishrag on her head, 2002. Just like her Papa Jack, she was always cleaning the house.

Our dog, Dusky, also known as "Roses," 13 years old, January 2002.

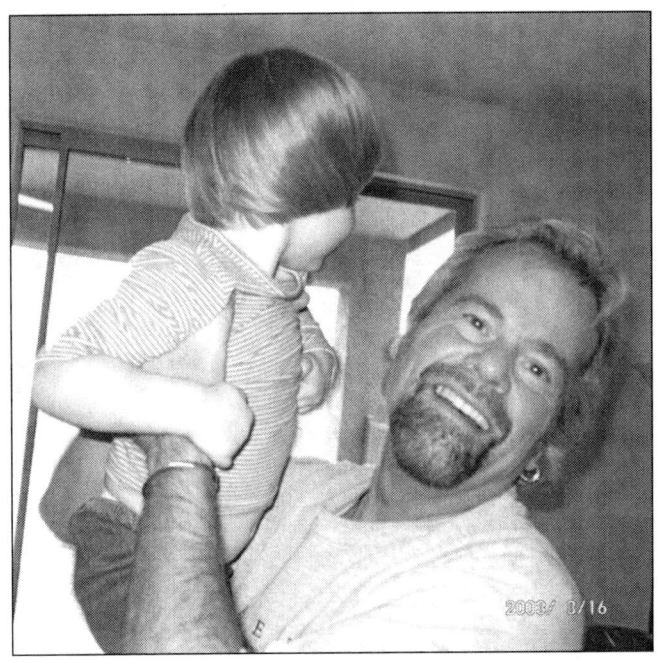

Madison, after getting another of Papa Jack's haircuts. Jack had exclusive rights to cutting her hair.

Jack and me, on a Hawaiian cruise, August 2002.

"We must be getting younger." My beacon of hope and me, sailing south on Lake Hamilton. Norway, Michigan, 2002.

Jack, on a cruise stopover in Key West, Florida, June 2003.

Jack and me, on a cruise, June 2003.

Tom, 35 years old, and Madison, 4 years old, early 2004.
It's obvious Tom is My Banana Bread Man's son. I miss being able to look into his eyes to see Jack's essence.

What he was continues to grow in what he left behind. "Death cannot steal what the heart knows."
Madison and me, 2004.

Weaving tales, rich and wild, as he did your hairstyle, in Jack's Self Indulgence, April 2004.

When Jack became ill, our night-blooming cereus cactus began to mourn; it went dormant.

Two and one half years after Jack's death, our cactus began to bloom again.

Our untraditional family was traditional in every sense of the word, Christmas 2003.

Back row: My mother Luciana Davis, Tom, Jack, my father Richard Davis. Front row: Me, Madison, Karrin.

Our friend Judi (from Michigan) and me, in happier times, early 2004.

No other friend or family member provided as many consecutive days of hands-on, in-depth, care as she did. This was a true act of love.

Jack and his nail tech, Brenda, at the back door of his salon, April 30, 2004.

Jack told her "I will always be your soft place to land."

Me, Jack, and my sister Cathy, at Crater Lake, Oregon, on the last trip Jack and I took together—a fitting and beautiful end to the life we shared, August 2004.

Jack, on the Oregon coast, five weeks before he received his brain tumor diagnosis, August 2004.

Me, on the Oregon coast, August 2004.

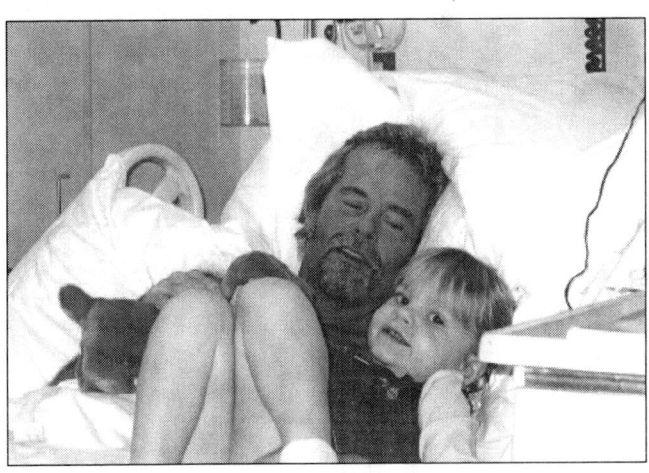

Jack, 55 years old, and Madison—Jack's personal ray of sunshine—4 years old, on October 2, 2004, the day he received his diagnosis. Madison always glowed for Jack.

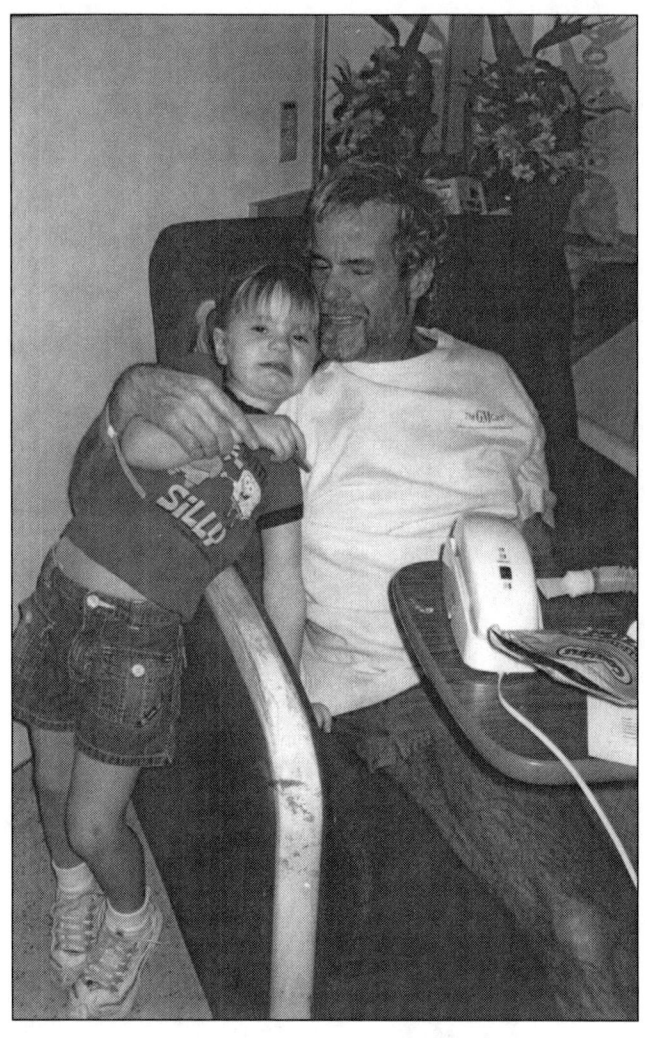

Jack and Madison, three days after his first surgery, October 9, 2004.

Two weeks after this photo was taken, a fall, followed by a stroke, coma, and hospital blunder darkened Jack's world forever.

Timmy, our Angel of Mercy.

A family still striving to be whole, after Jack had already had four surgeries and suffered a stroke, Christmas 2004.

Back row: Our friend Jerry, me, Jack, our friend Paul.

Front row: Luciana and Richard Davis, Karrin, Madison, Tom.

"But the only hope I had was one that would not be—for your brown eyes to open up and once again see me." Jack and me, Christmas 2004. The shunt running from Jack's brain to his abdomen is visible.

Jack, just prior to his last release from the hospital, mid-March, 2005.

"I saw a strong and gentle man begin his final race
I saw him fight the ravages of cancer's ugly face
I saw him live each moment of his last days on this earth
I saw him draw his final breath for all that it was worth
I saw the winds of time and spaces carry him away
I saw the angels coming, they would not let him stay."

Reflections

Writing This Book

I wrote *Finding My Banana Bread Man* to not only tell the story of Jack's difficult and painful passing, but to also pay tribute to the grand way he lived, his approach to life until he drew his last breath. While I wrote I realized I was using an amazingly powerful tool to rediscover, redefine, and find Jack. This comforted me and sustained my connection to him.

I also wrote to share with readers what I learned while I grieved for Jack, both before and after his death, because society does not know how to grieve. And grieving is necessary! I aim to help people grieve, so I share:

That anger, denial, fear, and pain, as well as hope, joy, laughter, progression, and, ultimately, acceptance are equal partners in the dying and grieving process.

My conviction that healing comes from remembering loved ones, not from burying them in the past.

The importance of establishing a legacy for loved ones.

The process I went through to forgive others and myself. It took a lot more work to forgive myself.

The healing power of the written word, the means I used to find My Banana Bread Man.

My joy in knowing that because Jack existed I am different than I would have been otherwise.

I share my firm belief that Jack travels into tomorrow with me, that love never dies.

About Brain Tumors

Dr. Peter Nakaji—a magnificent surgeon, who's on the leading edge of brain tumor treatment—saw to it that Jack received every surgical treatment available. I will always be grateful for his extraordinary talent and his dedication to saving Jack's life. I know he wanted to do more, but ... .

Dr. Nakaji's mentor Dr. Charles Teo says: "We do not keep brain tumor patients alive any longer than we did 50 years ago. If you've got a malignant brain tumor in an adult, then it's 100 percent mortality. Even though it ranks only about No.9 in incidence, it's the third most important cancer in terms of impact on society. It affects people in the prime of their life, it debilitates them so they are taken out of the workforce and it kills them at an early age."

In her book *Another Day in the Frontal Lobe,* neurosurgeon Katrina Firlik says: "Some neurosurgeons dedicate their careers to these tumors, looking for alternative strategies to outwit them. Their work has led to some creative options, such as thin wafers of chemotherapy [Jack's were called "Gliadel" wafers] that can be left along the edges of the brain where the tumor was removed. Logic might dictate that this should greatly prolong the time to recurrence, but the results have been less than stellar. Clearly, a breakthrough solution will have to be radically different from the options we have now, and it's probably not going to involve surgery."

Jack's cancer was a random, unlucky, and biological occurrence, and that was how his doctors described it to us. No one knew where it came from. It had no cause that could be linked specifically to Jack, although we speculated vinyl chloride—a chemical used in hairspray prior to its withdrawal from the market in 1974—might be the culprit. Research indicates there are beauticians who have been negatively affected by exposure to this chemical.

When asked if this could have caused Jack's tumor, no doctor was willing to state a possible connection. (I'm sure even if they suspected it, they would never commit to making what could be perceived as a libelous statement.)

The only explanation I was able to garner from the medical community was Jack's cancer was the result of chromosomes 19 and 20 gone mad.

Firlik states this about brain cancer: "I'm confident that a GBM is not retribution for any sin or misspent life (it would probably affect more than just fifteen thousand people per year if it were). In short, a brain tumor is the fault of no person or thing. As with a deadly hurricane, nature is both powerful and indifferent."

Was Jack's cancer, as Firlik says, "indifferent"? Yes, indifferent to whom it picked as a victim. It preyed on anyone, even healthy people like Jack. He took extremely good care of himself, better care than anyone I know.

Was the cancer powerful? Oh my, yes, like nothing I have ever seen. This disease diminished movement in Jack's left side. (He also lost his sight, but I personally don't attribute this to cancer, but to hospital misjudgment.) It literally stripped away mental pieces of who he was, and it played games with his cognitive skills, seeming to enjoy jerking them away so he'd have to struggle to get them back. This vile cancer scattered and hid in his brain, then silently assaulted and destroyed it.

I think the battle between man and brain cancer could be recorded in a best selling thriller or blockbuster film. The fight is real life played out before your eyes, and none of it is pretty, but, even so, it's worth looking at this cancer's modus operandi, so that you know getting it isn't anyone's fault.

I appreciate the hard work surgeons are doing to fight brain tumors, but it angers me when I see treatment hasn't advanced much over the last 50 years, and that the survival rate hasn't improved, either. I don't understand how the most powerful country on earth can make zero progress. Is this possible? Apparently, yes. What a shameful medical legacy.

Brain cancer isn't a popular cancer; funding research isn't important. Attorney Johnny Cochran and Tug McGraw—country singer Tim McGraw's father—died because of brain cancer, as did Gene Siskel, but I guess not *enough* high profile people have died to make a difference to "funding gurus."

What will it take to get them to raise money to battle the scourge of brain cancer? How many more people will have to lose their "Jack" before our political leaders decide it's too many? I don't know.

I am angry Jack was taken from the people who loved him. He may only be one fatality among many, and I may only be one small voice, but I intend to do what I can to raise awareness of the pain and suffering caused by this brutal cancer. I want something do be done to cure and, eventually, prevent it!

I hope by writing this book I will, in some small way, light a fire under influential people who can expose brain cancer for what it is. A killer.

(To learn more about Dr. Teo and Dr. Nakaji, go to abc.net.au/austory/transcripts/s841714.htm

To learn more about Dr. Teo's work, go to smh.com.au/articles/2003/03/09/1047144875103.html

To learn more about Dr. Katrina Firlik, go to katrinafirlik.com)

My Wish List

I found this "wish list" on the Internet. It succinctly states many of my wishes.

My Wish List
(Author Unknown)

I wish you would not be afraid to speak my loved one's name. They lived and were important, and I need to hear their name.

If I cry and get emotional when we talk about my loved one, I wish you knew that it isn't because you hurt me: the fact that they died causes my tears. You have allowed me to cry, and I thank you. Crying and emotional outbursts are healing.

I will have emotional highs and lows, ups and downs. I wish you wouldn't think that if I have a good cry, my grief is all over, or that if I have a bad day, I need psychiatric counseling.

Being bereaved is not contagious, so I wish you wouldn't stay away from me.

I wish you knew all the "crazy" grief reactions that I am having are normal. Depression, anger, fear, hopelessness and questioning of values and beliefs are to be expected following a death.

I wish you wouldn't expect my grief to be over in

six months. The first few years are going to be exceedingly traumatic for me. As with alcoholics, I will never be "cured" or a "formerly bereaved," but will, forevermore, be recovering from my bereavement.

I wish you understood the physical reaction to grief. I may gain weight, lose weight, sleep all the time or not at all, develop a host of illnesses and be accident prone, all of which are related to my grief.

Our loved one's birthday, the anniversary of their death and the holidays can be terrible times for us. I wish you could tell us that you are thinking of us and them on these days. And if we get quiet and withdrawn, know that we are thinking about them, and don't try to coerce us into being cheerful.

I wish you wouldn't offer to take me out for a drink, or to a party; this is a temporary crutch, and the only way I can get through this grief is to experience it. I have to hurt before I can heal.

I wish you understood that grief changes people. I am not the same person I was before my beloved died, and I will never be that person again. If you keep waiting for me to "get back to my old self," you will stay frustrated. I am a new creature with new thoughts, dreams, aspirations, values and beliefs. Please try to get to know this different me—I'm the one who'll be here from now on.

While Your Loved One Is Still with You

Smile and laugh together. When pain threatens to overshadow all that's good, hunt for humor; latch on to every opportunity to feel joy.

Talk a lot, then talk some more; reminisce about your shared past and all the good times you had together.

Touch. Your loved one *needs* touch, your touch.

Be yourself, the person you always were, and encourage your loved one to do the same. This is not the time to pretend.

Cry together. Comfort one another.

Acknowledge that your loved one is dying, and talk about it with them. They, and you, need to come to terms with their mortality.

Say "I love you" in as many different ways as you can, with words, actions, expressions, and touch.

Be an advocate for your loved one; they will not always be able to make decisions for themselves, so they need your help.

Write about your feelings and what you are experiencing. Keep a journal. This will become your most valuable tool for helping you grieve.

Record as many details about your loved one as

you can. Even though they are ill, and you think you won't want to recall this painful time, do it anyway. Record their voice, take photographs, make videos. These "living" symbols will help you grieve.

Say "I will remember you forever." One of a dying person's greatest fears is that they will be forgotten. The best gift you can give them is reassurance that they will be remembered.

Be there when they die. Move in close, and whisper in their ear that you love them, that you will always love them.

After Your Loved One Has Died

Write in your journal. As you begin your life without your loved one, you will find that the pen will become your most integral counseling tool.

Memorialize the one you lost through scholarships, donations, art, and so on.

Perform tiny deeds of good action in their name.

Remember them. Do not allow anyone to make you feel you should forget them. "They are tucked inside that special place that mind and matter can't erase. Death cannot steal what the heart knows."

Be the gatekeeper of their legacy. Keep their essence alive through what you say and do. "Even death's attempt to break you cannot separate what made you."

Turn to nature. You will repeatedly find your loved one's spirit here, speaking to you through a gentle breeze, the sunlight on your face, or "in the hummingbird's sweet song."

Dream. Pay attention to your dreams, because your loved one will visit you "while you sleep between these worlds."

Cry. Tears are an expression of the deep pain caused by losing the one you love; tears will help you.

Face their death. Do not run from it. "No time will heal the heart and soul of someone on the run." Deal with all the emotions: anger, denial, fear, remorse, regret, guilt, anxiety, sorrow, depression, and hostility.

Talk, talk, and talk still more. Find someone who will allow you to talk about your loss and who is willing to listen and listen and listen while you repeatedly recount your story of pain and your loved one's death.

Accept mistakes. You will make mistakes along the way; it's human and normal. Remember that you did the best you could under the circumstances.

Forgive yourself. Absolution is never instant; it's an ongoing process that you may return to again and again until you succeed.

Forgive people who have hurt you or who seem to abandon you; moreover, recognize that forgiveness will take time. If you cannot forgive someone, put their infraction aside, then return to it later. If you don't return to it, your feelings will fester inside you and inhibit your healing process.

Roles within families and friendships may change. Be prepared for this. The roles your loved one played in your life may not be easily filled by anyone else, or may never be filled.

Accept that you will lose contact with some friends and family members who are unable to grasp how your loss has invaded your entire being. Their loss is completely different from yours. "Some will say you can't let go, gentle hearts that think they know. Those who do not understand have not been to this dark land. Your recovery spans a lifetime. Theirs is measured in much less time."

Remind yourself that love survives death. Your loved one remains with you. "Love creates a bridge of joy that even death cannot destroy. Death becomes what can be seen, but you have memories of green."

Sending News to "Jack's Gallery"

Throughout Jack's illness, many friends and family members stayed in contact with me through visits, telephone calls, or the Internet. I wrote e-mail messages, to keep as many people as possible informed about Jack's status. I wrote my own e-mails, but you might consider appointing one or two people to do this for you. Your friends and family want to know how you and your loved one are doing.

Here is an example of an unedited e-mail message I sent to Jack's Gallery. Don't worry about writing perfectly; it's not important in these times:

> Subject: Update on Jack
>
> Good Morning to all of you,
> Since I last sent you a message Jack's condition as slowly worsened. He did have a wonderful birthday celebration on 6-15-05—then a day later he had a seizure—the end result of that is he is now bed bound. He had another seizure or small TIA on 6-27-05. We thought after that we might lose him by the middle of July—but his will to live has seen him make a remarkable turn around from that event. He appears to have rebounded from that seizure/TIA—so for the moment we are treading water.
>
> Jack is much more delusional since his last

seizure/TIA on 6-27-05—but talking and interacting with us all very well.

Obviously the overall situation with Jack's health is not promising and we know that at some point the cancer will take his life—we just do not know when—it could be tomorrow—it could be later—but we know his time is slowly running out. Any future seizure or TIA could present us with the life-ending process, which we wish we could avoid, but that we know is inevitable. His brain seizure medication has been increased, however, sooner or later, it will have no affect on the process—and he will be taken from us.

I realize that all these words are difficult to read—believe me they are even more difficult to write. Many of you have taken time from your lives to come and visit Jack and I cannot begin to tell you how much your gift of time has meant to him. No—he does not look like the same person you all knew—but his warm and loving personality is there for all to see, if you have the strength to visit with your friend. I will not thank those who have given Jack this gift of time—here—since you know who you are—and you will be forever changed for having spent this time with him. Every time I leave the room, kiss him goodnight, and have any interaction with this man I have shared my life with, I realize it may be the last time he may recognize my voice or know who I am. Time is not on your side if you are delaying any interaction with Jack—so if you are contemplating involvement you would need to do it now—not later.

I may attempt to "rejuvenate my batteries" for a short time at the end of July and early August (5-7 days). If this is possible I would put Jack into Respite Care for this short period and then bring him home, where I still expect to be able to care for him. If I am able to take a few days away I will drop you all a short note to let you know where Jack is staying. Due to his blindness and medical problems he may not really realize where he is during this short time frame—but I will not be there—so any visitors for Jack during his stay in Respite Care would be greatly appreciated. I want to make things as normal a possible, for him, for that period. The period I have in mind for the Respite Care is 7-27-05 thru approximately 8-2-05. You will hear more from me as this time approaches, and if it is even possible—Jack's health and stability will determine any time I take away from his care.

Once again many thanks to all of you who have sent messages of support, made phone calls, prepared food—but most of all to you who have come to visit Jack, and who "Jack Sit" for me—and involved yourselves in this a most difficult journey. Soon Jack will not be here to remember what you have done for him—but I will—and your acts of kindness and involvement in this process will remain with me forever.

Thank you, John—Jack, too

Requesting Help

Throughout Jack's illness, I often relied on "the kindness of others" for physical and emotional support. I learned to ask for help, stating specifically and thoroughly what I needed, like I did in this unedited e-mail message written only days before Jack died.

> Good Morning to Everyone,
>
> I am putting together the plans to place Jack in Respite care for a one week period from Wednesday (arrival time between 9 am to Noon) 7-26-05 through Wednesday (Departure time 9 am to Noon) 8-3-05.
>
> He will be at THE FORUM—Pueblo del Norte at 7090 E. Mescal Street in Scottsdale Arizona (Skilled Nursing area). The major cross streets are Shea Boulevard and Scottsdale Road (NW corner). Mescal Street is just North of Shea and West of Scottsdale Road. The phone number to this facility is 480-948-3990.
>
> I am trying to arrange a schedule of people who are interested in visiting Jack during this time he will be in this facility. **Visitors would be most welcome during this time.**
>
> If you are interested in signing up for a block of visiting time please CALL ME so that can put your name on a schedule for a specific time. By doing this I can ensure that visitors to Jack are

spread out over this time frame. If you wish to visit Jack during his stay at this facility I am asking that you select a time frame from the schedule below (any date, Wednesday afternoon 7-27-05 through Tuesday evening 8-2-05) and call me so that I can put you into your selected slot. After I have a list of names and times I will send you all the list prior to Jacks arrival on 7-27-05. (Note: please call me by Noon 7-26-05, so I have time to put the schedule together and get it all to you) If you plan to visit please maintain the selected time so that we can "keep him in company" during the time I am away. Even though the schedule below is in two hour intervals that does not mean you have to spend this entire time with Jack, even short visits during a selected time would be appreciated.

Many of you have asked in the past, "What can I do to help?" THIS IS IT—please visit him during this one week time that I will be away. I can't tell you how this will easy my mind—just knowing that he will be kept company by his many friends and family.

Select any of the following 2-hour time slots on any date 7-26-05 through 8-2-05:

9 AM—11 AM
11 AM—1 PM
1 PM—3 PM
3 PM—5 PM
5 PM—7 PM
7 PM—9 PM

This facility is open for visitors before and after the hours listed above, so if the above schedule does not fit your needs, just indicate that to me when you call to schedule your visiting time. I just assumed that the above time frames would cover most everyone's needs.

Again, please call me with your selected visiting time so I can put you on the list. You will hear from me again when I have the list put together.

Please give a copy of this e-mail to anyone who does not have e-mail access and would like to participate in visiting Jack.

You will hear from me again once I put the schedule together. Of course these plans are all subject to change if Jack's condition should worsen.

Many thanks to you all,
John

Caregiver Instructions to Helpers

Ensuring that Jack was properly cared for was of utmost importance to me, so when I needed help, I spelled out exactly what I wanted done. This helped keep Jack comfortable, and it gave his caregivers/visitors a clear idea of what they could do for him. People are more likely to volunteer if they know what's expected of them.

> Sent: Tuesday, July 26, 2005 11:21 AM
> Subject: Re: Update on Jack
>
> Here is Jack's Visitor Schedule for when he is at The Forum, Pueblo del Norte 7090 E. Mescal, Scottsdale, AZ, from 7-27-05 thru 8-3-05. JACK WILL BE IN ROOM # 211. Jack will leave home sometime between 8-9 a.m. on 7-27-05. I would assume he would arrive at the facility no later than 10 a.m. on that date, 7-27-05.
> Thanks to all of you who have signed up to come and visit Jack during his time at Pueblo del Norte. I know there are others who are waiting to see which openings remain and are planning to try to visit during those times to help fill up Jack's schedule. Thanks to all of you, as well, for all your efforts.
> A few items worth noting:
> If you happen to be there when he has been

given his breakfast/lunch/dinner, please assist him with eating. The facility that Jack is at feeds all of its patients in the dining room. Since Jack is bed bound, he will not be going to the dining room, so what they do is place the food in front of him and tell him (like a clock) where the food is. Then they check on him later to see how he managed. I know that this will not work for Jack, BUT I have no way of changing their policy. I know they will have a mess each day to deal with; however, my concerns have fallen on deaf ears. So if you happen to be there during feeding time, please assist Jack with his meal.

I will be sending a lot of snacks with Jack. They will be in the room. When you're there please offer to get him some of these snacks to eat.

Since he is blind, he cannot see you, so be sure to tell him who you are and touch him on his right side. (His left side is severely impaired and he cannot feel your touch on that side.)

Jack will be getting a massage every day he is there, except Sunday. If you happen to be there when the massage person is, you DO NOT have to leave; you can still talk to him as this is happening. The times for this will probably vary day to day.

Sometimes Jack will have his eyes closed; that does not mean he is asleep. Just talk to him; he should respond. If he is asleep, please wake him. Your visit is more important than his sleeping.

Sometimes he floats in and out of a conversation; just keep talking, he will enter the conversation when you least expect it. And he probably hears everything you are saying.

If you are going to see Jack, I assume you are a close friend/family/customer, so please give him a kiss when you arrive and when you leave—tell him one of these is from me.

Two people, I and Jack's son, Tom, will be called in the event of an emergency.

If you ask any of the staff at Pueblo del Norte how Jack is doing, they are only allowed to say "fine"; they cannot provide you any details. The only people who will be allowed detailed information about Jack are me, Jack's son Tom, and the following two people, Marion Reitmeyer and Sharon Kagan.

Analogy for Grief

(I posted this on the Grief Healing Web site)

I thought of something last night, which, for me, is a perfect analogy for what is happening inside a grieving person. Pretend, for a moment, that someone pulled out all the electrical wires and plumbing in your house, your perfectly built house.

From the outside it appears as if nothing is wrong. It still looks whole, and the outer shell still has its pretty paint on it, and the landscaping in the yard remains untouched. (Many people don't see the shambles you're in because from the outside you appear to be normal.) But when you try to live in your beautiful home, you have trouble; you have no electricity and no water, not because electricity and water aren't available to you, but because they are not connected. Your house is a shell. What a dilemma.

How will you fix it? Do you want to fix it? You wouldn't want to bulldoze it because the shell is still perfectly good. You would have to access its insides, the deep insides, the place covered by walls and plaster. You'll have to have the wiring and plumbing reinstalled, and it could take months of painstaking work to be sure everything works properly, and, in the meantime, you will have to live in an empty shell and make do with what you have.

For me, this is what grief is like; my "shell" is still here, but all my internal wiring/plumbing has been ripped out and damaged, and it must be reconnected if it is going to work again. Reconnecting is a slow and difficult process because I desperately want to use my old wiring and pipes—memories of Jack.

I have most of the old materials, but they have become a large tangle of wire and pipe, and I have to find a way to adapt them to work with new wires and pipes. My job is to salvage what I can and make it work. To become fully functional will require I manipulate new wire/pipes until they correctly join with my old ones.

I begin the process of reconnecting, taking it one room at a time, because I really love all those wires and pipes that appear to be in such shambles, and because I can visualize what my house (the person) will again look like—if I give it enough time.

Somehow, at some time, this project will become reality. The lights will burn again, and the water will flow. I hope they burn brighter and flow faster than before.

Letter from Papa Jack to Madison and Mia

One of Jack's prized possessions was his collection of 12 Hummel eggs. I felt his granddaughters would benefit from receiving it, so I decided to give them one egg every Christmas until they've received them all. Here's the letter I enclosed with the first egg, the Christmas after Jack's death:

Dear Madison and Mia,

Hello, Sweet Babies. This is Papa Jack writing to you. Please remember I am always with you and I love you, even though you cannot see me.

Madison, Mia is too young to understand the gift in this box, so it will be your job to tell her about it: who it is from and what it means.

As the years pass, this letter will begin to mean more, so when you're older go back and re-read this letter each Christmas: it will all become clearer to you as the years go by. Each year at Christmas, when you get an Egg from me, take this letter out and read it, then remember I am always with you.

I loved these Eggs; they were part of a collection I started 10 years ago, and I want you and

Mia to have them. Papa John will make sure you get one Egg each year. After 12 years you and Mia will have all 12. As you grow up you will both have these Eggs, a part of me.

After you have received all 12 Eggs you should each choose six to keep as your own. Remember me, remember that I am always with you. Whenever you look at these Eggs, think about how much I love you. Madison, by the time you receive all 12 Eggs you will be 17 and Mia will be 12; by then you will understand how much I loved you and how much I will always love you and that I am always with you.

I will not be here, in person, to give these Eggs to you. My body stopped working, and I had to leave. Please know I did not want to leave. But always remember that whenever you feel love I am with you. It will be Mommy and Daddy's job—Papa John's job, too—to tell you all the stories about me and how much I loved you and how I am always with you. Even though you cannot see me, I am always with you, and I love you.

I am with you when the sun is shining on your face.

I am with you when you look at the Christmas tree and see the shining lights.

I am with you when you fall asleep at night and when you wake in the morning.

I am with you when you're playing, riding your bike, or coloring pictures.

I am with you when you're dancing, eating, or just walking with your friends.

I am with you day and night.

I am with you right now.
I am always with you.
I love you, Madison and Mia. I am always with you.

                            Love, Papa Jack

Dream: Leaving to Accept

I have had this recurring dream, which is finally beginning to make sense to me. Jack is not in it, although, I think he can teach me things without appearing in my dreams.

The dream relates to when I was working in Michigan with Unemployment Insurance (UI). I was continually presented with people in a situation called Leaving to Accept (LTA). It was a process we went through when a person left one job to take another.

Based on the law, I had to determine how long the person could have continued working at the former job and how long he was expected to work at the new job, and then calculate unemployment benefits. There was no penalty if they increased the length of their employment when they left the first job and went to the second job, meaning if they left one job and had another job waiting, they were expected to remain employed at the second job longer than they were at the first.

If they are laid off, they might be eligible to collect unemployment without a reduced payment (a penalty). If they leave one job and take another, knowing they will be employed less time than they were at the first—in construction work, for example—their benefits were affected. This was always one of the most difficult concepts for me to learn, but, even though I had a hard time with it, it eventually became second nature for me to apply the rules properly.

I think my dream is trying to point out several things:

It was difficult to understand LTA, but I eventually learned how to use it. Leaving to Accept seems to be much like what I am going through now. The grief process is excruciating for me to deal with, but I will eventually catch on and properly apply and incorporate it into my life.

Jack had to leave life to accept death, just like I had to let him leave, and now I have to accept his death.

I should ask myself the same questions about Jack's death that I did when I was working these hard UI cases. At work I always had to ask the first employer, "How long could this person have continued working had he not left your employ?" Then I had to ask the second employer, "How long was he expected to work at the time of hire?" So now, I guess, I need to ask myself, *How long could Jack have stayed had he not died? How long is he expected to stay where he went?*

The answer to the first question seems obvious: He could not stay any longer; his poor body had been used up. The answer to the second question is also obvious: He is expected to remain there indefinitely.

When I put it this way, it all seems to make more sense. He had no choice about where he went, and neither did I. There is no penalty applied for Jack leaving because life is always shorter than death.

Jack performed properly during his first assignment (life). Now it's my turn to recognize this, and recognize that these are the rules of life—as hard as they are to accept, so to speak. I have to accept his leaving.

I have to understand and accept the phrase, used in my prior job, as it applies to life: We all eventually Leave to Accept.

My Father's Box

I wanted to share with Tom my memories of my life with Jack so he could combine them with his own. I prepared "My Father's Box" for Tom, which included this letter and all the items listed. I want Jack's granddaughters to look through it when they are older. It was quite a job to get it together, but it was worth it.

Tommy,
In this box, "My Father's Box," are all the things that represent your dad's life and what he loved. When you look at them they bring back memories of who he was and what gave him joy throughout his life.

So many of these items are just little things, but, when taken together, they truly give a sense of who he was, what he did, and how he lived his life. Open each precious piece of memorabilia, then keep it as a constant reminder of that wonderful man you called Dad. Always keep My Father's Box of memories, pass on to your children the story of each item as it relates to you. This will keep his memory alive and provide you with comfort.

Your dad loved so many things. Things like:

- Lemon Curd and "Winto Greens," and Cherry Kool-Aid and Windmill Cookies served simultaneously
- I Can't Believe It's Not Butter and honey graham crackers
- Anything with cranberries or blueberries in it, but cranberries were his all-time favorite flavor—unless he was eating lemon curd straight out of the jar
- Jell-O, especially pistachio, cherry, or raspberry
- Altoids breath mints and "tooth pickers," which he also called "Shep pickers"
- Vitamins and herbs; he was crazy for anything new. If there was a new "snake oil" being sold, he was first in line
- Drakkar Noir cologne and lotion, Gleem—only Gleem—toothpaste
- Caress and Dove soap, Neutrogena Bath Gel. He loved brand names. He wouldn't use generic
- Contact lenses, Carmex for his lips. Only Carmex
- Sunglasses. Expensive ones, like Serengeti; nothing cheap
- Phones—landline and cellular. I often told him it seemed he should have a phone growing out of his ear
- Cars, especially Cadillacs—he owned seven—and car shows
- Tires for his cars. He loved to get new tires. Does this sound familiar?
- Home shows. When there was one in town we had to go
- A McDonald's Quarter Pounder with Cheese meal, a Diet Coke—he watched his weight
- Movies and movie popcorn on a Saturday or Sun-

day night, or Friday or Monday afternoon. He would cry at sad movies. He would also tell me he loved me

The movie "Pretty Woman"; it was his all-time favorite. He would watch it anytime. And Bruce Willis. If he was in a movie, we had to see it

Anything that Patsy Cline sang; she was his favorite singer. He was very romantic and loved her love songs

Pillows. Lots of pillows—in bed and around him. They must have made him feel warm and secure

Hairdryers and mirrors and hair dye and clippers and scissors and combs and brushes and ... the customers who went along with all these things

Arizona summers. Thanksgiving and Christmas, too. He loved these two holidays. I always gave him one Christmas present as soon as the tree was put up. He always got one or two new Christmas ornaments each year—usually a Hallmark—and nothing cheap

Anything and everything to do with family, friends, and dachshunds. He really loved Dusky

Your dad just loved Life.

But the things he loved most in life will not fit in this box, nor is there any box big enough to hold all his precious love, since most of all he loved ... You and Me.

I Love you, Tom.

Letters to Jack

I started writing "Letters to Jack" on September 30, 2005, two months after Jack died. These letters gave me a way to continue to speak to him while I adjusted to his physical absence; doing this gave me a way to forgive, express anger and disappointment, sort through my thoughts, and channel my grief. Writing helped me recognize Jack's spirit when it landed in that soft place in my heart.

Good Morning Jack,
I started the day in tears again. Many of my days start like that, but today was particularly sad, and I'm not quite sure why. The pain is as fresh as if you had just left.

I hope you know how much you are missed by me, how much you were a part of every piece of my life. It is a pretty empty "me" that was left here to go on. Somehow I have to find a way to put all those sad images of you—when you were sick—in their proper place so that I will remember all the wonderful and colorful years of our lives together. I wish I knew how to bring all the good memories to the surface and let the painful ones sink.

Perhaps you could tell me in a dream; you

have done a remarkable job, so far, with the kind messages you have given me in the dreams you have sent my way.

I have tried to stay busy; even did a little yard work. I clean the house and keep everything in order. I do all these things, but they are just tasks without you to share them with. I really miss sharing my life with another human being, and, since I know I can't ever share it with you again, I would like to do it with someone else. Do you think that would be ok with you? I know, I know, you have already given me that answer many times. We always told each other that we would want the other to "go on," to live again, if something happened to one of us, but we probably thought the one left would be very old.

So here I am at 55 trying to "go on," to live again. How I wish I could do this all with you, but I can't. But you can come with me, tucked away in my heart and in what I say and do.

I know I have to let you go to be able to move on. It's kind of like not being able to walk if you're hugging someone. I think I have been hugging you since you died, and that was wonderful when we embraced, but our hugs, in life, had a beginning and an end. All I'm really saying is that I need to end "this" hug so that we can find the future. We can both then walk together and find our proper place, AND we can hug again, but we'll do it so that we can hug and then let go, to walk again. Please know that will not mean I love you any less, but that I love you even more. I think I need to let you find your place in my memory, in my heart, a place that is comfortable for you. Find a warm and loving place and let me wrap my arms around you there. Hug you there. It can be your place forever, and it will be one that you have chosen and that I will protect for you always, and one that I will visit for hugs often.

I'll be carrying you with me wherever I go, whatever I do. That "you" I knew and loved so much will always be with me. There is a great deal of you in me that still lives, and I will love you forever.

I will let you go, so that I can keep you close forever.

Until we hug again, I love you more than you will ever know. Lots lots.

        Your John Boy

I desperately needed forgiveness, Jack's forgiveness, for my countless shortcomings and for the inadequate ways I cared for him during his illness. I later learned that many caregivers have these feelings.

I also sought self-forgiveness. My hospice counselor Ann Hamlin suggested I write a "Good vs. Bad" letter to Jack and list all the bad *and* good things I did.

> My Dear Jack,
> Sometimes I think that I spend a lot of time remembering the bad things that I may have done during the time that I took care of you. I've had one of those days, I've been beating myself up—so I have decided to make a list

of the Good vs. the Bad and see what the list shows—I hope this exercise and letter to you will help.

BAD:

There were times when I would get upset when I was cleaning you, or when you would not follow my instructions to stand. I know we seemed to start almost every day with a verbal struggle, before you became bedridden. I should have known better—but I did not—I feel bad about this. I know I usually apologized when I did this. Please know how sorry I am for my shortcomings.

One time, when you would not swallow your pills, it felt like you were biting me, and I tapped you on your cheek, scolding you not to bite me. I should have known better—although I did not recognize it—your illness was causing you to chew when you thought you were trying to swallow. I am so sorry.

I should have spent more time just sitting with you when you were in the living room (and could walk) and then when you were bedridden. Sometimes you just wanted to sit and talk; sometimes I did that, and other times I did not. The only excuse I have is that I needed to try to keep busy doing other things. I was almost crazy with watching you slip away from me. I wish I had sat there and been with you all the time; but I also know that caregivers need to pull away. Despite knowing that, I still feel bad for not spending more time with you.

Sometimes you had so many requests during a day that I would get short tempered when "another request" was made. I should have been more understanding; after all, you could not see. But I did apologize many times, perhaps not as often as I should have. For those times I did not, please know I am sorry.

I did tell you I was going to put you in a home when you bit me. I hope you know that was out of frustration; there was no way you were ever going to go to a home other than Our Home. And that is where I kept you until you died.

GOOD:

I made all the meals, except those brought to us by friends. I think I became a halfway decent cook—especially breakfast—you said that my breakfasts were great.

I fed you when you were not able to feed yourself, and I remember really enjoying being able to help you with this. I cooked the best I could, and you seemed to enjoy eating, even though you were ill.

When you had to pee I held the urinal for you—and you did have to go to the bathroom a lot. Just the way your system worked. You peed often, even when you were well. LOL.

I gave you showers daily when you were able to stand up, and then gave you sponge baths in bed when you were bedridden. This included cleaning your bottom.

I took you to the bathroom whenever

you needed to have a bowel movement. This was pretty labor-intensive when you could still stand. I may not have been as patient as I should have been, but we got the job done.

I kept your briefs and pads clean when you were bedridden—everyone from hospice told me I was doing a good job at this. I had no experience, but I sure tried hard.

You had many requests: Winto Greens, or drinks, or popcorn, or a comb, and I tried to get you all the things you needed. I know sometimes it was overwhelming (the requests were many), but I really did try my best.

I shaved you almost every day, some days I missed, but, for the most part, I got this done.

I scratched your back as often as I could, when you asked.

I massaged your legs and kept them elevated when you had a swelling problem.

I kept the house clean; this kept me in busywork, so I could escape mentally from what was happening.

I paid all our bills and kept all the financial items in order.

I filed for your Private Disability Policy and for Social Security Disability, and got all that money coming in. What a load of paperwork.

I kept all the hospital paperwork straight, and tried to share all that with you so you would feel on top of your medical treatment. This was difficult sometimes, because the fact that you were blind and the nature of brain tumors caused you to have delusions. This complicated how we interacted.

I sold my truck and then took out a HEL and bought your car. So much paperwork when there were other greater concerns, but somehow I managed.

I wrote tons of e-mails, trying to keep friends and family aware of what your latest condition/problems were. I made tons of phone calls—and you know how I hate the phone.

I was able to keep the yard work done and everything trimmed. Thank God we have mostly desert landscaping, and all of it on a watering system.

I extended the pool warranty and dealt with problems with the pool. God, I hate that thing.

I took you on walks outside and down the street, when we were able, and then, when you could not walk, in the wheelchair. It was not often that we could go, but when I had help we did.

I kept you home for the entire time, and you died at home. I remember telling you a number of times—maybe more—that I was going to keep you home, that I would always take care of you, not to worry.

When you could still walk, especially in December and January, we would go in the car for appointments, and to the Arizona Council for the Blind, even out to eat. This was labor-intensive—walking you to the car, getting in and out—because you were blind. It was hard on both of us. It is really amazing what we were able to do.

When possible, we went on social outings: to Tom's house (Xmas and Thanksgiving and Easter), to my parents', to restaurants. We tried to make this as normal as possible, despite the nightmare we were both living in.

I got you all your pills—and kept track of them. The hospice people seemed to be pretty impressed with the way I was able to keep track of your medication.

I helped you through three seizures, the last one just before you died, when I had to give you a Valium enema to help stop it.

I called 911 two times—once in October, when you went blind (I am sure I saved your life), and again in January, when you had one of your seizures. I know you might have thought it would have been better to die, but I am so glad that I had something to do with saving your life. At least I was able to have you with me for a while longer. As hard as it was, I treasure the last 10 months I had with you.

I organized your 56th Birthday party. What a blast we had. You said it was the best BD you ever had.

I wrote your eulogy and planned your "Celebration of Life" while you were still alive. I knew you were going to leave me, and I had to be prepared. I wanted it to be the best eulogy and "Celebration of Life" ever. It was hard for me to do this when you were still alive and with me. I think what stopped me from involving you in these plans was you seemed to forget that you were dying, and I saw no point in reminding you about this; after all, the nature of your illness and blindness seemed to make your circumstances different than the norm. Yes, you should have been involved in these processes, but with what was happening to you, I think it was best that I handled them for you.

I made the decision to stop having you take your "chemo" drugs. As hard as this was for me, I think it was the right decision, and I'm putting this in the "good" column. Giving you more chemo was possibly causing your immune system to create more problems, like the warts. I knew you would not want to live longer if the quality of life was not there. So, rather than keep you alive for me, I maybe let you go a short time earlier, **but I did that for you**. Jack, this really was an act of love. I hope someone does the same for me.

I was your advocate, for the entire time you had to be involved with the hospital and medical community. I fought for you "tooth and nail." I'm sure many of these folks thought I was insane, but I wanted the best for you, and when my perception was that you were not receiving the finest care, I was "in their face." I ensured that you had the best there was to give.

Now that I have finished writing the Good vs. the Bad, I think I feel better. Yes, I did things that were not nice, kind or considerate, but when I look at what I did that was good, I believe the scales may be tipped to that side.

I have had a rough day today; I was dwelling too much on the 5 Bad things and not the 29 Good things that I was able to identify here.

I'm very sorry for the 5 Bad things, but I am also proud of the 29 Good things that I accomplished during this last 10 months of your life. **I love you as never before.**

Your John Boy

When your loved one is dying, you might forget to let them know that you appreciate specific things about them. After they die, you might think it's too late to tell them, but you can still accomplish this via a letter to your loved one. Once again, this is "the power of the pen."

During my grieving, I felt it important to thank Jack for the things I'd neglected to thank him for when he was alive. The next letter is my extended thank-you to Jack.

> My Dear Jack,
> Thank you for:
> Moving to Arizona with me. That was not an easy thing for you to do; to give up your Michigan customers and move here. I know you ended up indicating it was the best thing you ever did, but that initial decision was not easy. You adjusted well to everything we ever did as a couple. Thank you.
> For that wonderful trip to the Grand Canyon, in 1985, with Tom. What a blast we had— a real time to remember. Remember how we sold our hotel room to eight Chinese people, when we

decided not to stay the night? You were such a character. Thank you for this, my darling.

For giving me Dusky as a birthday present, in 1989. What a gift. That was one of the nicest gifts I have ever received. A real gift of love. All the years of joy he gave to both of us. Thank you for giving me Dusky.

For that surprise trip to Milwaukee to see Cathy in a play, in 1989. Wow, I was really surprised! You always did such kind and considerate things for me. What a treat. Thank you.

For all the new cars and trucks you insisted that I buy; you always wanted me to have a new vehicle. Money was never an issue with you, only making me happy—and you did. Thanks for each and every one of these vehicles.

For buying two houses with me in Arizona and the one back in Michigan. We had so much fun fixing each one up. We were good decorators. I never told you, but together we had a real flare for decorating and making a home one that "hugs" you when you walk into it. **Thank you, my love.**

For pushing us to get rings after 21 years; I should have been more aggressive in pushing for this myself, and I don't think I really properly thanked you for ensuring that this symbol of our love was made a reality. Thank you, Jack. I now have these rings as that symbol of our unending love. What a gift!

For all those numerous swims we had in the summer evenings following our walks. You sometimes had to drag me out of my chair to do the walks, but I am grateful for these special moments; they are a wonderful memory, and your initiative to move me along made it all possible. A sweet memory, indeed.

For the movies on Saturday, or Monday/Friday afternoon, or Sunday, with the popcorn; what a treat these times were in our relationship. Then when we could not find a movie we wanted to see, we would do a DVD at home on a Saturday afternoon, with Dusky eating popcorn between us. These were some of our greatest times together, all three of us. I keep our popcorn bowl as a special memory of this good time.

For all the trips between 1995 and 2004—so many to Palm Springs and San Diego. Oh, how you loved Casa de Bandini—and the Mexican food. I never truly thanked you for all these wonderful trips we made together and the great times we had. All the car trips in which you would lay back and read the papers and I would drive, then we would switch, and these were good times, and thanks for making all these little moments special. You were fantastic at "living in the moment," and I failed to recognize that wonderful quality in you. What a great life you lived. Thank you for showing me how to live a good life.

For being the best partner and lover anyone could ever have; you were the "best of the best." I did not tell you as much as I should have. **You were the best and only person I would have wanted to spend the last 27 years connected to. Thank you.**

Others' Words About Grief

My grief often went beyond my words; at those times it was helpful to read others' words on grief. This led me to collect quotes. Some people collect them in a scrapbook, box, journal, or jar, and then, from time to time, pick one to look at. Here are some quotes I collected.

"Things have a terrible permanence when people die."
—Joyce Kilmer

"All the photographs were peeling
And colors turned to gray
He stayed in his room with memories for days
He faced an undertow of futures laid to waste
Embraced by the loss of what he could not replace"
—Eddie Vedder: "Sad"

"When the rain washes you clean you'll know. You will know."
—Stevie Nicks: "Dreams"

"Where you used to be, there is a hole in the world, which I find myself constantly walking around in the daytime, and falling into at night. I miss you like hell."
—Edna St. Vincent Millay

"When it is dark enough you can see the stars."
—Charles A. Beard

"Normal day, let me be aware of the treasure you are. Let me learn from you, love you, savor you, bless you before you depart. Let me not pass you by in quest of some rare and perfect tomorrow. Let me hold you while I may, for it will not always be so. One day I shall dig my nails into the earth, or bury my face in the pillow, or stretch myself taut, or raise my hands to the sky, and want, more than all the world, your return."
—Mary Jean Irion

"Life begins on the other side of despair."
—Jean-Paul Sartre

"Beauty that dies the soonest has the longest life. Because it cannot keep itself for a day, we keep it forever. Because it can have existence only in memory, we give it immortality there."
—Bertha Damon

"He who learns must suffer. And even in our sleep, pain that cannot forget falls drop by drop upon the heart, and in our own despair, against our will, comes wisdom to us by the awful grace of God."
—Aeschylus

"His noble face is more alive to me now than any of the faces of the living, and in his eyes I always see that light of transcendent wisdom and transcendent compassion that no power in heaven or earth can put out."
—Sogyal Rinpoche

"Hope is the thing with feathers
That perches in the soul
And sings the tune without words
And never stops at all."
—Emily Dickinson

"I've been fortunate enough to borrow from everyone else's experience. I've seen people in every state of neurological decline and I've seen death, over and over again. And this makes me feel lucky about life, every day.

"As I think about this, I have to admit that my appreciation for the everyday has become a well-entrenched part of me now. I probably don't need constant reinforcement."
—Katrina Firlik—Neurosurgeon

"The only truly dead are those who have been forgotten."
>
> —Jewish Saying

"God gave us memories that we might have roses in December."
>
> —James M. Barrie

Victims or Victors?

Knowing what I now know about the devastating strength of GBM tumors, would I have wanted Jack to pursue the treatments he did? Would Jack have chosen them? I don't think so.

Jack always met problems head on; he thought he could conquer anything he set his mind to, including cancer. Nothing was insurmountable. If I had been the one who was ill, I would have felt the same way. (Perhaps we lived together long enough to take on each other's problem-solving strategies.)

But, try as he might, Jack couldn't conquer the cancer that attacked him. Had we known this was going to be the result, we would have chosen six to eight weeks of good health and certain death over seven surgeries, blindness, and ten months of pain. Knowing death was imminent, I think those six to eight weeks would have been all the more sweeter.

That being said, we wouldn't have settled for eight weeks together if there were *any* chance we could have years. Despite statistics to the contrary, we always believed we could beat this monster, and in some ways Jack did beat it.

Cancer wanted to take away all that he was, and he refused to let it succeed. No, he didn't conquer the cancer in his body, but it did not conquer him—

or me—either. Instead, it provided a vehicle to take me back in time so I could recall and record the spirit of who Jack was before he became ill.

As I've said, cancer could not take away Jack's essence from me, even though it stole his physical presence. I found ways to memorialize, remember, and create Jack's legacy; I found ways to help other people threatened by illness and early death.

Jack knew how to live and how to die. I now know how to live on to tell his story and learn from it, how to move forward, and how to remember. Are we victims or victors? Victors! Definitely!

Individuals Named in This Book

Jack (Jackie O): Partner of John (deceased 7-31-05)

John (John Boy): Partner of Jack, Scottsdale, AZ

Dusky: Jack & John's dog (deceased 12-6-04), Scottsdale, AZ

Dolly: Jack's mother, birth name Clarice, Norway, MI

Luciana & Richard: John's mother & father (father deceased 8-29-07), Scottsdale, AZ

Tom: Jack's son, Norway, MI

Madison: Jack's first granddaughter, Norway, MI

Mia: Jack's second granddaughter, Norway, MI

Karrin: Jack's daughter-in-law, Norway, MI

Cathy: John's sister, Ashland, OR

Barbara: John's sister, Green Bay, WI

Timmy: Friend of Jack & John (deceased 7-03-06)

Judi: Friend of Jack & John, Hamilton Lakes, MI

Sharon: Friend & neighbor of Jack & John, Scottsdale, AZ

Brenda: Friend of Jack & John, Fountain Hills, AZ

Pattie: Friend of Jack & John, Fountain Hills, AZ

David (number one): Friend of Jack & John, Norway, MI

David (number two): Friend of Jack & John, Niagara, WI

Lanette: Friend of Jack & John, Glendale, AZ

Penny and Marion: Friends of Jack & John, Phoenix, AZ

Paul and Steve: Friends of Jack & John, Scottsdale, AZ

Paul and Jerry: Friends of Jack & John, Phoenix, AZ

Ron and Dave: Friends of Jack & John, Phoenix, AZ

Larry: Friend of Jack & John, Scottsdale, AZ

Ray: Friend of John, Phoenix, AZ

Roy: Friend of John, Toronto, Canada

Mick: Friend of John, Scottsdale, AZ

Ann: John's hospice counselor & friend, Phoenix, AZ

Lorraine: One of Jack's hospice volunteers, Fountain Hills, AZ

Shep: One of Jack's hospice volunteers, Scottsdale, AZ

Marty: Individual who wrote the Foreword, Phoenix, AZ

Dr. Peter Nakaji: Jack's neurosurgeon, Barrows Neurological Institute, St. Joseph's Hospital and Medical Center, Phoenix, AZ

Dr. Frederick Marciano: The neurosurgeon who informed Jack he had a GBM tumor, Barrow Neurosurgical Association, Ltd., Scottsdale, AZ

Dr. Katrina Firlik: Neurosurgeon and author of the book entitled *Another Day in the Frontal Lobe,* Greenwich, CT

Acknowledgements

Jack should have died on the morning of October 23, 2004, but he didn't; he stayed with me for nine more months. For this, I am grateful to him; his survival created this story. I am also grateful for the hope and love that resulted from my efforts to write this book. Every second of despair, loss, anger, fear, regret, guilt, depression, and hostility that evolved during this struggle gave way to hope and love; therefore, hope and love are acknowledged as intangible elements that helped carry this story to its ultimate end.

Beyond Jack, hope, and love, there are many who played pivotal roles in making this endeavor possible. Were it not for my core supporters, I would not have survived. I offer my immeasurable gratitude to my Angels of Mercy—my sister Cathy, my parents Luciana and Richard, and my dear friends Judi and Sharon—who helped steady the hand that wrote these words.

The friendship and support offered by Lanette, Brenda, Ann, Ray, and Roy allowed me to reconnect to life at a time when I didn't know connecting was an option. During the darkest days, they helped guide me along a path to recovery, and they share responsibility for me being able to write this book.

The list of names of other friends, family members, and Jack's former customers, who played a role in this story, is voluminous, and to include it here would double the pages of this book. That I can make this statement is a testament to Jack's popularity and the throngs of individuals who, in kind and gracious ways, assisted us during his last year of life.

I wish to thank my mother Luciana, my sister Cathy, Sharon, Estelle, Brenda, Judi, and Roy for their advice and counsel about the contents of this book. Their efforts greatly assisted in its completion.

The content editing of this book was completed by Faye Quam Heimerl, who, in the course of this venture, became my good friend. Upon reading the original manuscript, she asked me numerous probing questions, which then allowed me to expand the breadth of my message. She was able to twist and shape the contents of what you have just read and provide seamless movement from words to poetry. I treasure my connection to this gifted professional.

In addition, I feel a debt of gratitude to Tom—Jack's finest creation—and his first granddaughter Madison, who provided Jack with years of pleasure and love. Beyond me, I can think of no other individuals who provided him with such joy. Many of Jack's finest attributes were enhanced through his interactions with them. They are shining examples of many of the qualities he possessed. They hold the ability to carry his legacy forward, and to ensure he will never be forgotten, because they are, in many ways, the mirror image of who he was.

I love Tom and Madison for what they meant to

Jack. Tom was a wonderful son to his father; Madison was a wonderful granddaughter to her Papa Jack. I love them for who they are as individuals and for making a difference in my life. I also love Mia for who she is to Jack: an infant born after his death, but whose existence at conception was known by him. To me, she will always be Jack's namesake, sweet little Jackie O.

Finally, I would like to recognize the committed and loving relationship Jack and I shared for 27 years. It was a communion of two souls who genuinely loved and cared for each other.

Even death's attempt to break us
Will not separate what made us
I may not see and hear him say
That he loves me every day

Love creates a bridge of joy
That even death cannot destroy
He may not be in my sight
But his love visits every night

This unique and treasured partnership guided my hand while I created this book, and it will guide the remainder of my existence.

About the Author

J&J, "A Real Item." Jack—Jackie O—and author John R. Davis—John Boy—partners in a committed relationship for 27 years.

Before becoming an author, John retired from a career with Arizona's Unemployment Insurance Program.

John resides in Scottsdale, Arizona, where, in loving memory of his Banana Bread Man, he dedicates his life to helping others who have also suffered the premature death of their spouse, mate, or partner.

To comment on *Finding My Banana Bread Man*, or to invite John R. Davis to speak about his Journey Through Mourning, please contact John at FindingMyBananaBreadMan@cox.net. To learn more, go to FindingMyBananaBreadMan.com

LaVergne, TN USA
19 July 2010
189920LV00001BA/2/P